The Mexico Solution:
Saving your money, sanity, and quality of life through part-time life in Mexico

– by Kerry Baker

Illustrations by Karen Ferreira

Dedicated to

Robbie Monsma, who has been with me on this all the way.

Acknowledgments

Thank you to the beta-readers/editors for their kind trudge through the redundant drafts.

Kerri Atwood, Laurie Brodeur, Karen Brown, Steven Melbye, Robbie Monsma, and Mike Wyrostek

Table of Contents

Introduction

"I'm not going to Mexico to live forever. I'm going to go there for a while to see if I can recreate a life that closely approximates what I had in the U.S. on half the budget, instead of moving to a featureless small town in America. I'm not looking for a "cultural experience."

—Journal entry, April 14, 2014

The road along the Malecón opened up unexpectedly, miraculously, to an open stretch for miles ahead. Alejandro, the Uber driver, stomped on the gas. Flying down the beachfront road, I squealed, "Que libertad!"

"Si," he answered with his gaze fixed in front. "Hay que aprovechar." —Journal entry, July, 2015

Getting From There to Here

Admittedly, Mexico was not my first choice. In 2009 I had a traditional game plan of moving to my dream American city—in this case Denver, Colorado—getting a reasonable if not perfect job, saving the prerequisite 15 percent a year, making some friends, and living my life.

Five years go by. In a dream I am at a pool and responsible for a bird, a bright red parrot that for some reason I was supposed to take for a swim. I wasn't supposed to hold it down in the water too long. Then it got dark. I couldn't find the bird, and it drowned. I woke up crying, thinking the dream meant that I couldn't take care of anything. A dream-interpretation book said that dead birds signify the death of a dream.

What was dying were my plans for the future. After job hunting unsuccessfully in the three industries I knew, I was out of ideas. Even in tight labor markets, job prospects for those over forty-five are bleak without specialized skills, skills I didn't have. Mexico made sense as a place to tread water, even if only part of the year, and save money while I figured out the next step.

When well-meaning friends suggested that maybe I should move and try to find a job in a cheaper town, my heart stopped; I was scared more by the thought of moving to a suburb of Dallas than by moving to a country whose people did not speak English. I saw the years laid out before me . . . shopping malls, a lot more mascara, and a landscape as flat as an HD television. I could imagine almost every day of the rest of my underfunded, overworked, anxious life, and the "tyranny of indistinguishable days."

To further encourage me in my job search, a friend wanted to introduce me to a woman she knew, a former IT professional who had just gotten a new job at age sixty-four. She rode bikes competitively, my friend enthused, demonstrating that with vitality, all could be overcome. "What kind of work does she do now," I inquired. She had taken a position with a furniture store. Oh, I thought, furniture sales isn't so bad. "So does she like sales?" I asked. "No," said my friend, "I think she's a back-office clerk."

A number of people with good intentions who love you will be very happy to steer this kind of tiny life to you. Usually they have never been in anything like your shoes. They do not have to live with your choices.

In Mexico, there is an enormous moth, the Black Witch Moth. It can be the size of a small plate. The condo I rent on the ocean in Mexico is nothing but windows on two sides. One afternoon I found one of these moths beating desperately against one of the windows on the inside. You've seen it with birds. You can feel their panic and confusion.

You try to capture it to take it to an already open window, leading to a wild chase around the room as you attempt to help the terrified creature out of what must be a horrific situation in which they, for good reason, hold you suspect.

You see the scene played out all over Mexico, people hanging from ledges fifteen feet off the ground as they try to open windows for the behemoths. Restaurant servers knock over the furniture trying to catch and release them while the poor things hide inside lamps and behind blinds.

This time, however, as I extended my hand to the moth, it walked onto my palm and remained there as I walked it all the way across the large room to the open window. I could feel it trembling in my hand, taking the risk, being braver than the rest of the moths, sensing perhaps that it did not have a choice but to do something different. If it were to have a chance at regaining its freedom, it needed to find an open window.

Members of America's middle class have good reason to be tremble a bit. But fear has a long history of providing the impetus to create a more interesting, innovative lives.

Many people in the U.S. millions probably, believe that Mexico or another less expensive country is in their future, a way out. While this book is geared towards those who want the best of both worlds, the potential part-time expat, its chapters cover many practical and cultural aspects of moving full-time to Mexico (cooking, making friends, learning Spanish, cultural adjustment). The sharing economy and technology have opened the window to amazing choices on how and where to live.

As a person researching part-time expat life rather than moving to Mexico permanently right away, I got exhausted by having to sift through all the information relative only to full-time residency, such as buying a house or certain car issues, raising fears that only served to gaslight my expat ambitions. This book substitutes that information with that specific only to part-time expat life, such as how to rent out your U.S. place for the periods while you're gone, instead of drowning you information about Mexican driver's licenses and your housekeeper's employment taxes you might need later.

Many books and articles have been written that cover the facts about Mexico's top expat destinations and "how-tos" about moving and living in Mexico. Most ignore the emotional magnitude of living in a foreign culture. I have sought to capture through personal anecdotes points that many articles make only by telling you " life is slower," "you need more patience," "you have to be more flexible," and that "the people are warm." When I was researching Mexico, in addition to the mechanics, I wanted to know what those types of statements really *meant*. I hope my stories will demonstrate how those rather banal words translate into your daily life in Mexico.

Admittedly, these anecdotes reflect my ride, a modest and middle-aged ride, rather like riding the last small, yet still entertaining, waves to shore. Regardless of the intended scale of yours in Mexico, I believe you should expect similar experiences of cognitive dissonance, cultural bonding, comic misunderstandings, sensory delights, and irrational fear.

If you suffer from a life that is daily becoming more expensive and routine (in that unique way that staying on one shore can), part-time expat life might just be the balance between the known and the unknown that you're looking for.

Chapter One: Is Mexico dangerous?

News of how dangerous my life is in Mexico always comes unexpectedly. The first time, a few months after my arrival to Mazatlán, a friend called me from Denver to tell me how brave I was to live here. At the moment of the call, I was sipping a piña colada. I was walking to the beach near El Cid Marina on the north end of Mazatlán. I stopped for a moment and looked around to make sure she wasn't seeing some threat through the phone.

The next time it happened while I was watching the sun set over the ocean from my place and listening to Juanes sing "Es por ti" (for probably the fiftieth time). Another friend called to tell me she had decided not to come visit me. Mexico was too dangerous.

Answering the question of whether Mexico is dangerous is a no-win topic that I would love to skip. People who think it is (dangerous) are usually impossible to convince otherwise. Those who believe it is not more dangerous, like me, are equally adamant, as well as defensive. If I ignore the question, I am sure I will be accused of hiding the truth or being naive. The topic, like Trump creeping around behind Hilary Clinton in the 2016 Presidential debate - quiet but impossible to ignore. My editor suggested that I get it out of the way quickly so we can move on.

I will confess that I, too, fell victim to a certain degree of irrational fear before considering a life in Mexico. Like most people, I read the stories and gave equal credence to every source until realizing that the people to listen to were the people who knew the country and the people who actually lived there. Colorful, violent stories will always have more legs than the happy, sunburned recounts by any among the thirty-five million annual visitors and one million-plus American expats who live in Mexico (and probably as many illegally.)

I love my uncle who lives in Denver. Yet when twelve people were killed and seventy injured in an Aurora theater in 2012, I did not call him and suggest he leave Colorado. Conversely, when narco-traffickers are killed anywhere in the Mexican state of Sinaloa where Mazatlán is located, in neighborhoods expats would never find themselves in, I am invariably sent a news link.

Part of the problem is that people look at State Department travel advisories only once they decide to travel. If they had instead paid attention to the advisories over time, they would see that the advisories have remained pretty much unchanged for the last ten years. The State Department has revamped its guidelines from years past however, switching to Level 1 through 4 advisory alerts, Level 1 being the safest. Level 2 is "Exercise increased caution due to crime." Sounds pretty ominous, right? A number of tourist destinations, including Cancún, Cozumel, Baja, and Mexico City often can be found in Level 2. The language in these advisories about Mexico even scares me, and I know better.

To put things in perspective, Level 2 is the same tier of advisory given to the United Kingdom, Belgium, and Italy - places many of us would think nothing of traveling through. Mexico is not the safest country, nor is it among the most dangerous countries. Like the U.S., Mexico falls in the middle. According to NationMaster.com, which uses UN-based data, Mexico does not make the list of the thirty-five nations with the highest murder rates.

Glasgow, London, and Napoli, Italy top the list of most dangerous cities in all of Europe. Would a tourist even check a travel advisory before going to London? Sophisticated travelers realize that whether they are in the dangerous city of Detroit or the dangerous city of Juarez, the chances of anything happening to them are still statistically slim.

It is not that Mexico does not have problems with violence. The problem is that what you read in these general travel advisories creates a sense of alarm so completely out of proportion to the truth about Mexico as to render them ridiculous. Advisory reports lack the nuance to make them valuable.

Mexico's most crime-ridden places are not expat destinations. In fact, many major U.S. cities, including Baltimore, Detroit (unofficial, yet proud motto: "Detroit: Where the weak are killed and eaten") and Washington, DC, have much higher murder rates than any of the cities an expat is likely to visit, much less live in. The U.S. assault rate is five times higher than Mexico's. Mexico's violent crime rates for assault, kidnapping, and rape, are substantially lower than Canada's. State Department advisories measure violence differently for Mexico than they do for Canada or Europe.

When things happen in another country, we perceive it differently than we would events in our own country. I recently read a very typical article in *Business Outsider* noting with great alarm that narco-related violence appeared to be drifting into tourist areas, highlighting a recent killing that happened a mere *five miles* from the hotel zone.

I once lived in one of the nicest areas of Richmond, Virginia, the Fan, less than three miles away from Gilpin Court when a family was massacred in 1994, and just across the James River from where the Harvey family was murdered in their home in 2006. Drugs drove the murders in both cases. *The Richmond Times Dispatch* did not publish any pictures of those murder scenes. Mexico's press would have. Mexico's reporters do not do the country any favors by showing pictures of decapitated people hanging from bridges.

I lived in New Orleans' Garden District for a year too. New Orleans is fabled in every type of literature from vampire novels to mystery-detective books. It is like having a foreign country tucked away in America's South. New Orleans is one of the only places in the country where some natives speak a different native-American language - Creole. Its food heritage is distinct and unsurpassed. It is a fascinating city, and a dangerous one.

Outside of New Orleans, you are unlikely to see stories about the high level of crime in the city, violence that has continued from my time there to this day. The FBI reports the murder rate of New Orleans is declining, but it is nearly four times higher than all of Mexico and over five times higher than Mexico City. Yet, murders in New Orleans do not make national news the way a murder in a Mexican tourist area does.

The State Department does not issue travel advisories for the United States. Given that the U.S. has a higher intentional homicide rate than Turkey (Level 3), Lebanon (Level 3), Burundi (Level 3) and Cuba (Level 3) — and had 323 mass shootings in 2018 — well, let's face it: America is a Level 2 country. If the U.S. issued reports on itself in the same sweeping terms we use for Mexico, giving warnings over entire states where violence occurs, it would read like this:

Travel Advisory - United States of America

Due to recent violent activity, travelers are urged to avoid the following areas: The states of Nevada, California, Texas, Florida, and Pennsylvania. Outdoor concerts and athletic events such as marathons are also to be avoided. Extreme caution is particularly advised near schools....

Another likely source of people's fear is *availability bias*. According to availability bias theory, a person will latch onto and form their opinions based on information that is easiest and most available, rather than researching the topic from reliable sources. Often the most available information is anecdotal—a colorful, emotional story you read in the paper or that a neighbor shares with you.

For example, a student hears an unnerving story from a friend about a college girl getting drugged at a Mexican resort. This story is the most easily available information she has on Mexico. She cancels her vacation to Cancún. I personally know two women who have been drugged in trendy bars in Denver. I have plenty of other information as easily available about Denver to balance that against. The logical conclusion should be that women everywhere need to watch their drinks, not that they should avoid Denver, Colorado or the entire country of Mexico.

Even we expats on Mexico's expat forums are not immune to availability bias, becoming self-proclaimed experts of the entirety of Mexico, forming opinions about areas of Mexico we have never lived in and know nothing about other than what we, too, have only heard about anecdotally.

After so many of these discussions, I have finally reconciled myself to the fact that, for many people, researching the facts or even talking to expats will never be enough. Once you investigate the city that interests you through people who live there or have spent substantial time there, including talking to Mexicans, you will learn what every expat already knows: that all but a few areas are as safe as any decent-size city in the United States or Canada. You will also come to find that Mexico is a darn big country.

Energy generated by fear can either freeze us or free us. Change and leaving the zone of the predictable is uncomfortable. We have to do it though because personal growth stops when change stops, and you can't have change without moving something around. Fear has the same power over you whether it's warranted or unwarranted (as it is here). You can use fear (such as fear of 2,000$ MRI screenings) to drive you, or you can let fear dictate and narrow your life's parameters the way most do.

Travel Between Cities and Towns

One pleasant sunny Saturday afternoon, I decided to accompany a Mexican couple I am friends with to El Rosario, a little tourist town less than an hour outside Mazatlán. My friend wanted to visit a well-known homeopath whose office was on the main street of the town. On the way, as we wound through a road lined with a half dozen varieties of mango trees, they casually remarked that sentries involved with the narco-trade were probably monitoring the road. Later, after a delicious lunch, she casually mentioned our needing to be back on the road before nightfall.

One of the most endearing features in America's cultural landscape is its romance with the open roads iconized by Route 66, road-trip movies (*Thelma and Louise*), books *(Fear and Loathing in Las Vegas)*, and the drag-strip culture of its heartland.

I once drove my red 1966 Mustang in -106degree temperatures from Virginia Beach to Altus, Oklahoma, alone, over two days. I lost two cowboy hats out the window and picked up two German hitchhikers. The sole condition was that they keep me awake, since by then I'd been driving over twenty-four hours. This they accomplished from the backseat with poetry recitation and German drinking songs.

For all of us who are used to this kind of interstate freedom and the transformative quality of the road trip, the caution one should take traveling between some cities in Mexico can be unsettling. Travel in Mexico between certain cities or towns requires a little homework you would never think about doing in the United States. These smaller towns, like Mexico's *Pueblos Magicos,* are wonderful places to visit, and you should not be discouraged from doing so. Just do it during the day, like Mexicans do.

Greater Personal Freedom

One evening a Mexican friend of mine stopped by to drop off a gift from his wife before returning to Guadalajara. After chatting a while, he suggested taking a drive around the city. Having raised three children there, he knew Mazatlán intimately.

Once on our way up the Malecón, he thought of a view of the city he wanted me to see. First we stopped off at a restaurant, where he asked the server to bring us two beers to go. We then arrived at our destination and parked the car on a steep hill. We walked up the uneven, elevated, steep, cracked sidewalks in the dark, during which time my friend repeatedly alerted me to the air conditioning units and wires hanging out over the sidewalk in front of me.

As we climbed the road up the hill overlooking the city, he scanned the street until he found a private home under construction. The security guard watching the property helped us pick our way through the half-built house in the dark until we were standing behind it. From a small patch of ground, we could see the lights of the city spread out before us, probably the most dazzling view in Mazatlán.

That was the moment when I realized that we were standing on the brink of a cliff in the dark, and drinking beers on private property with no protection or guardrails whatsoever for the price of a ten-peso tip to a security guard.

If you look rational and want you want to seems to make sense, Mexicans will generally go for it. You don't have to deal with the infuriating rules for the sake of rules as you often do in the United States. Lawsuits are much harder to initiate. People often say that Mexico is like the U.S was in the '50s. Mexico is more likely to treat you like a responsible grown-up and leaves it up to your friends, lovers, and family to treat you like a child. With far fewer rules come a smorgasbord of ways to get yourself in trouble.

In Mexico, one is largely free of what some view as draconian ABC laws (Alcohol and Beverage Control), redundant airport security measures and other inconveniences related to controlled access. With the greater freedom of movement comes an element of risk. The point is that yes, Mexico can be dangerous - just not for any of the reasons most people think.

Mexicans, who will always be more affected by crime than expats will ever be, do not consider illegal drugs their country's key concern. That spot is taken by corruption. From the Pemex executive to the local politician to the parent who pays a bribe to get their child into a certain college, corruption is the country's biggest challenge. This is far less likely to affect you than a Mexican.

Long-term expats in Mexico who read this will likely think even these tepid warnings are unnecessary. When you are new to a country, you are off balance. A little extra precaution is warranted in any unfamiliar place.

"Fear is a song that only knows one note, stop, played in an endless loop," said poet Julia Cameron. Fear is what keeps us from creating the life we really want. The best way to change the music that accompanies Mexico is to consider your sources, talk to people with direct experience, and get your reports from international sources.

Resources:

Nationmaster.com uses U.N. - based data to compare countries. You plug in whatever countries you want to compare and it gives you statistics on many categories, including crime. The differences in the reports between the U.S. and Mexico on those categories related to crime and violence will shock you.

The blog/website Two Expats from Mexico, written by a former Florida law enforcement officer, offers a number of tools and tips on his website regarding safety, common scams, consumer protection practices and how to research a particular area for crime.

If you are one of those who believes "the devil you know is better than the devil you don't know," Borderlandbeat.com is the place for you. It has the latest and goriest on cartel activity in Mexico (I am surprised by the number of otherwise normal expats who adore living in Mexico and still love to read this kind of thing). *Mexico News Daily* also gives crime news and is less graphic. For those who involve themselves in the drug trade, Mexico is very violent indeed.

Checklist:

- Don't panic if you see armed cars carrying masked soldiers bearing assault rifles and machine guns in your Mexican town. It does not mean anything is necessarily wrong.

Which would be more intimidating if you were a criminal: A policeman wearing a Kevlar vest carrying a sniper rifle and a machine gun, or one wearing shorts riding a bicycle? Same goes for security measures on display in houses in expensive neighborhoods. Barbed wired and clearly displayed elaborate security does not necessarily mean a problem with crime exists. It means the home owners want aspiring burglars to see barbed wire and elaborate security systems.

- Avoiding driving between towns at night – road construction hazards are common. Use toll roads (*cuotas*) when possible if you do not speak Spanish and are unfamiliar with Mexico. Make sure to have enough pesos to pay the tolls. While some toll booths take credit cards, a series of small charges on your card will trigger a fraud alert, disabling your card.

- When traveling and staying in Mexican hotels carry your own carbon monoxide protector.

- Use the same level of caution in Mexico that you'd use in any unfamiliar major American city (being alert to your surroundings, not drinking too much in bars, being polite). Add an extra dash of caution and courtesy if you do not speak any Spanish.

Chapter Two: Getting Personal - Making Friends in Mexico

Si te vas, yo también me voy

(If you go, I go also)

Si me das yo también te doy...

(If you give to me, I'll also give to you, love), amor

Enrique Iglesias, from song *Duele Corazon*

A thriving industry in Japan in the last few decades is that of family-member rentals. A person can hire a mother, husband, or grandson from agencies that send actors who play those roles for a fee. The client may hire the actor for one occasion, like a father-in-law for a wedding, or the actor's role may extend for years, like playing the role of a father for the child of a single parent.

As odd as that sounds to Westerners, only in the last century or so have family relationships in the West aspired toward the ideal of unconditional love. For centuries, family members played transactional roles. Children were another set of hands to work the farm. Women were married off to be mothers and caregivers first, with the hope that love would dutifully follow behind.

Our relationships are still transactional, especially our friendships. We must gain something from them. They must receive a benefit from interacting with us. Our friends make us laugh, think, or strive to be better people. We cannot change, improve or test our beliefs in a void. Friends and close acquaintances (friends in training) enable us to do that.

Before you go on to conquer mainland Mexico, you might want to spend some time building relationships with expats who know the places that interest you, preferably before you arrive, in order to get advice. Even one contact in a Mexican town can make all the difference. Most people initiate contact on social media, through Facebook, or by participating in expat forums. Every popular expat town has at least one Facebook page. Expats frequently post to forums (although it tends to be the same expats who post).

Everyone has their own way of making these types of connections. While I did not always have new ideas, I woke up every morning for a year before moving to Mexico asking myself what I could do that day to make some contacts with people already living there.

Once you are committed to making the change to a two-country lifestyle, ideas and methods of reaching out in keeping with your personal style have a way of opening up to you. The person with the Mexican connection might be a person at your gym or a neighbor on the elevator. Cast the net into every area of your life. By its nature, commitment to a plan stimulates the growth of special antenna that pick up information to help you reach your new goal.

I have never been very good at Facebook and social media networking. I met one couple who had a second home in Mazatlán through a hiking group. I questioned the skills of another friend whom I knew was great online networking skills and told her she'd never be able to find a contact there (She was too young to have heard of Huck Finn. Some of us make up for being old by being devious). Within a week, she introduced me online to a resident, literally a friend of a friend of a friend of hers, thereby retaining her crown.

In some ways, once in Mexico, it is easier to make friends than making friends at home. Walking into a bar or restaurant, expats automatically scan the horizon for the rest of the flock. As an expat, you are a legacy member of a special fraternity. It is almost awkward to stand in line behind an expat and *not* exchange a few pleasantries.

Expats depend on one another in times of sickness, emergency, and cultural bewilderment. Most expats do not have family in Mexico other than their expat family. This interdependence creates tight relationships and unlikely bedfellows.

In reviewing a journal from the first few months in Mexico however, I was surprised to remember that I did not want to spend more than a few hours a week with expats.

It was not out of any sense of superiority or aloofness. In a sincere desire to help, long-time expats are open fire hydrants of information, knocking you to the ground with the force of their knowledge. They will share where the best roast chicken is sold, their dentist's name and fee schedule, and the price of a bus ticket to Durango, all before you can find your way consistently to the nearest ATM machine.

It takes time to process it all. You need breaks from the uncurated torrent of advice you may or may not ever need. With such an onslaught, plenty of times I wanted to just hide out at a neighborhood taco stand, with only the soft sounds of Spanish around me.

My own timing in arriving to Mexico was fortuitous. During my first month in Mazatlán, I saw an ad for a housemate in the local online newspaper. Knowing I had a lot to learn about operating in the culture, this seemed like the perfect living arrangement for my first long stay. Plus her house was right on the beach. The surf crashed into her patio wall hard enough to make the whole house shake.

With her forceful stride, as she walked down the malecón to meet me The Intrepid Elise appeared a young doppelganger of one of my best friends at home. Blond-haired, blue-eyed and a former ice hockey player, I got a kick out of her authentic Mexican accent, and the surprised reaction she got when she flung it around. She had visited Mexico as a twelve-year-old, and right then and there, set the goal to live in Mazatlán someday.

At 21, she moved to Mexico from Vancouver with little Spanish. With her surfer-girl looks, she could have easily gotten a job in tourism, talking to North American vacationers all day. She opted for grueling restaurant work instead to learn the language. By the time we met, she had racked up several years of running her own property management company after managing a motel. She straddled a social life perfectly divided between Mexicans and fellow expats. I was in awe.

The Intrepid Elise coached me on electricity usage (electricity is billed differently in Mexico), gas ovens, and all manner of security procedures in a country where you always have to be vigilant of your stuff. We were housemates for five months. It grew into a casual business relationship, like being hired for a job after a frequently embarrassing internship.

Seeing her in action, I decided to take after her example. As a single person, I didn't want to limit my pool of friends to the small population of expats who lived in Mazatlán during the off-season, the months I had chosen to live there

At home, we try to figure out what potential friends might want from us and what we might have to offer them. Spoken or unspoken (and probably consciously and unconsciously), we strive to fulfill our end of the social transaction. Our role in a friendship usually encompasses sharing insight, humor, sympathy, and encouragement.

These sentiments are harder to convey without a good command of the language. In trying to make Mexican friends without fluent Spanish, I spent a good bit of energy trying to figure out what a Mexican could possibly get out of knowing me. What contributions might tide them over until I learned the language well enough to support them in their lives? How to go about making Mexican friends though, especially with very limited Spanish?

The answer came from observing a friend of mine at home - in my admiring view, an American Sniper of friendship-building. If she struck up a conversation with a promising person in a chance encounter at a festival or a hair salon, she focused - using the exact same approach you would for a potential romantic partner. She conducted individual campaigns, a much less exhausting approach than trying to be everywhere at once. Studies have shown that a friendship requires ninety hours spent together. My friend took pains to get together with that person frequently for months. Within a few years, she had a garden of close friends.

Focusing on only a few people works particularly well in Mexico because of the country's group culture. You will rarely meet a Mexican without a well-developed social and/or family network (and proceed with extreme caution if you do). In my experience, they are more inclusive, willing to invite you to join their groups faster than at home.

My first target in Mexico was named Lupita (as were the following two, making for some pretty confusing phone conversations). She was charming and authentic. She had an incredible voice, as lilting as a teenage girl's. She hosted a radio talk show on, of all things, human sexuality as it related to health.

On rare occasions, Lupita would attend a weekly language exchange group. Every week for months I went to the language meetups and hung out like a love-struck schoolgirl, hoping she would show. When she did, I'd jostle myself to sit nearby, practically ignoring everyone else at the table. She held my undivided attention. I complimented her incredible skin, her taste in clothes, and her voice. I was completely shameless.

Courting for friendship without being fluent in the spoken language is like being interviewed for an entire day. For two summers I would return home from the language practice meetings and pass out. Many a time my eyelids would droop from language fatigue as the other members in the group were warming up. But I never left until they did.

Why, you may ask, go through all this angst to make Mexican friends when it's so easy to meet expats?

Mexican friends, both those who speak English and those who do not, were the ones who taught me how to make flan and tortillas. They explained Juan Gabriel and Vicente Fernandez to me. They invited me to private cultural events, opera, and museum lectures where I was probably the only American in the room.

They donated their adult children to stay with me nights when I had a surprise hospital stay. They took me to views of the city only the locals knew about. Mexicans have been the best thing about living in Mexico. They made it home.

I discovered that once you make a Mexican friend or two, your social circle expands out to include sisters, husbands, children, and children's boyfriends/girlfriends. Little by little, you will likely be included at family gatherings occasionally or invited to special celebrations, like picnics in *el campo* or birthday parties. That's when you will really fall in love with Mexico.

In the meantime, I asked myself, how was I going to hold their attention until I had the language thing down?

September 2016

One evening while living in a condo in the old Pato Blanco Hotel in Mazatlán, I spied a group of friends, a mix of expats and Mexicans and some of their acquaintances, through the back of the foyer having an impromptu cookout by the pool. I approached to say hello, and they invited me to join them.

In the flurry of preparation before diving into the cheeseburgers and spread, I asked the person whom I knew best if there was anything I could do to help. He replied mischievously,"Don't be boring."

Don't be boring. So easy to say yet so hard to do. When you are living in another country and navigating a second language, the steps you typically take to "not be boring"at home are more difficult to access. A joke or off-beat idea may require third-tier vocabulary. Amusing nuance is harder to convey.

Humor often doesn't translate well. Invariably, another county's humor is deemed silly or childish by the outside culture. The thoughtful comment you want to make about a home's pre colonial architecture is reduced to the frustrating "You have a pretty house (*tu casa es muy bonita!*).

The challenge for me was speaking comprehensible Spanish while still demonstrating some vestige of a personality. Without Spanish, I was left with the most primitive of social tools. I smiled a lot without knowing what I was smiling about. I learned that facial expression, the one where only your eyes smile, that can move in a heartbeat to sorrow, humor, surprise or empathy when you are completely lost, rather like good dogs do.

My second summer in Mexico, whenever I waited for the water taxi to go to the gym, I worked on memorizing the fairy tale Cinderella in Spanish. In the Spanish version, Cinderella asks the birds to come pick out the peas that the evil stepmother has thrown in the ashes in exchange for her permission to go the ball. Cinderella directs the birds with the words:

"Las buenas, en el pucherito"

"Las malas, en el buchecito"

I had no idea what those lines meant.

It sounds like a drinking toast, though, doesn't it?

I thought so too! So one night with my Mexican girlfriends after we uncorked our first bottle of wine instead of the normal (boring) toast of "salud," I broke it out.

"Las buenas, en el pucherito"

"Las malas, en el buchecito"

I was gratified by peels of laughter. I don't think they knew what a pucherito was any more than I did. I explained where I got the lines and that became our official toast for weeks. I have used it several times with others and invoked the same hilarity each time. Out of context, it might even sound vaguely dirty, but it's Cinderella. What could they do to me?

When you memorize a story word for word, even complicated phrases will work themselves into your daily conversation. You might suddenly blurt out a sentence in irregular future subjunctive verb tense lifted from the memorization. People who were hearing you struggle with simple present tense two minutes earlier once again find you a rather surprising companion.

Jokes, quotes, and toasts are perfect little snippets of Spanish to use as icebreakers. They are great to memorize while on the bus killing time (usually waiting for the internet to come back). I got a lot of mileage out of that one Cinderella story.

Only a few weeks later, the same friends and I were passing under a flowering cherry tree well after midnight, coming out of a dance place on the beach.

The sidewalk lamplight shining through its soft pink translucent flowers created a sparkling and magical effect as we walked under its branches. I searched for an interesting remark. Coming up empty, I dramatically announced to my friends, waving my arms at the tree above:

> *"Arbolito, secude tus ramitas frondosas"*

> *"Échame oro y plata y mas cosas!"*

> (The quote from when Cinderella pleads to an abundant tree to throw her down a fancy dress for the ball.)

My friends were appreciative. I like to think even struck by my fervor.

The point is that when you live in another country, never be afraid to make fun of yourself or be overly dramatic when trying to make native friends. Memorizing a passage or making a funny toast in a second language takes effort. Mexicans know and appreciate that. If you can make them laugh from time to time, they will never turn you away.

As you stumble across interesting quotes or lines in English, do your best to translate them into Spanish. For example, from reading Oscar Wilde, I borrowed one of his quotes and used it as a toast as well: "To men with futures and women with pasts," to thoughtful approval. Even the shop-worn quotes I have heard a million times at home were new to my Mexican listeners and seemingly kept them satisfied until I could speak the language well enough to return back to my boring self.

Never say no.

I said yes to every invitation, no matter what my misgivings about a picnic in a cemetery or an outdoor party in a blaze of -95degree heat and one-hundred-percent humidity. Taking leaps of faith is a tough but gratifying phase of the expat experience as you establish a core mix of friends from a stew of expats, Mexicans who speak English, and/or native Mexicans who speak no English.

During year three, Lupita became comfortable enough with my stalking to invite me to a book club social held every other month (since I wasn't ready to discuss Tolstoy in Spanish). A year or two later, I got invited to regular book club meetings (I bought books in Spanish that I had already read in English, reported on them in Spanish, then donated the book to the club's library). At those meetings I developed my next great Mexican friendship.

Effusive, dramatic, and funny, entering each meeting like she hadn't seen the members in years, Estella and I shared a remarkably similar childhood considering one of us was a Mexican from Sonora and the other was an American from Altus, Oklahoma. We both left rural towns early to work in far away states. You may find in Mexico that you have much more in common with your Mexican acquaintances than you think.

The Two Biggest Mistakes You Can Make in Making Mexican Friends

Even in these days of texting, Mexicans like to drop by unannounced. The first big mistake you can make in Mexico is not answering your door when Mexicans drop by to visit. People tend to stop by late by American standards.

When I open the door of my condo, I never know how many people will be standing there. If a friend is picking me up in her car, I never know how many people will be sitting in the backseat when I open the car door. These are the characteristics that make Mexico special to me. This is a culture where children of the same sex usually do no have their own rooms, reflecting the inclusivity that endures all their lives.

The second biggest mistake you can make is giving even a hint that you need to go to bed on said evening. Do not, under any circumstances, ever, ever glance at your watch unless you never want to see that particular Mexican (or his family) again. Make a cup of coffee. Have a shot of tequila. Run in place. I know expats who proudly announce their bedtimes to Mexican visitors and wonder why they do not have any Mexican friends, believing it is because of their Spanish, when Mexicans are much more accepting of poor Spanish than we are of imperfect English.

Reputations have to start somewhere. I hosted little soirees *(veladas)* in the first year. I bought tickets to plays that I couldn't understand a word of. I picked up tabs for people I barely knew (a gesture no one can afford anymore in the U.S.—gone the way of meals on airplanes and drinks on the house).

I'm not embarrassed to admit any of it. I know that I got the better end of the deal. Even with all my efforts, it was hard to stay ahead of them because they kept reciprocating my reciprocation. Mexicans are kind and generous in a way that will take your breath away. Four years later, that circle of people made up the nucleus of my social group. Not only do I love them, I also feel safer in the country. If I have any doubts about anyone or anything, there are people, Mexicans born in my particular Mexican town, whom I can turn to.

Be who you want to be.

Anytime you move to another place, you have the chance to be anyone you want to be. As an expat, one comes to a new country without the baggage of the past. In a new environment, you realize just how much of what makes us who we are (or were) is based on our physical location, environment, and the people around us. Moving to another country gives us the opportunity to reconfigure who we are. Part of the reason to live in a new country is to take that opportunity to test out new approaches to life.

Focus on Mexican friends first.

Time with expats offers a tempting path of least resistance when a person is new and desperate for companionship. It will be harder to summon the extra effort needed to make true Mexican friends if you can always fall back on the company of expats.

Focus a majority of that first year enthusiasm and energy on developing a Mexican network. Think of expats as being like family you can always go home to, and Mexicans more like the new boyfriend/girlfriend who takes more effort but makes your life more exciting and memorable. Begin your courtship early. Mexican friends, expat friends. You need both *in* Mexico to get the most *out of* Mexico.

Maintaining Friendships at Home.

"I left you a message a week ago on Facebook. Didn't you get it?"

"Don't you have me in WhatsApp?"

"Can you Facetime me?"

"I sent you a message on Skype. You never got back."

"Sorry, I didn't recognize your Mexican number. It had a 52 country code so I didn't pick up."

"I can't call you on your MagicJack line, can I?

In addition to all these communication wonders, there is also my beloved 30$ Telcel flip phone, which I can drop it on any Mexican tile floor, watch it break into pieces, and put it back together like new. It fits in my *front* jeans pocket. It only has Mexicans' numbers. When my Mexican Bat phone rings, I know a Mexican is on the other end, which always makes me feel good about my Mexican Experience.

Interpersonal communication comes hard for me. I can be sitting around forlorn, thinking how much I miss a particular friend while a two-day old message from her sits unread in an in- box. I've improved over time, I hope, but it's another reason why I'm so grateful that Mexicans will still knock on your door.

While people may go to Mexico to escape technology, ironically it is technology that enables them to live there the most comfortably by still keeping them connected to home. Between all these tools and new tools that are always in the works, you can effectively maintain your American friendships while living in another country part-time. You just have to decide which tool is the preference of each of your friends (Not your preference – theirs. As the one who left, the unwritten rule is that their preference trumps yours).

As cities in the United States get increasingly expensive, people who love them are finding themselves pushed out. They often have to retire to smaller, less-expensive towns, leaving their established friendships behind for good, other than phone calls and maybe an annual visit. Five years ago, my choice was to either to move to a nondescript, cheaper American town and never live in the same city as my friends again, or move to Mexico part-time and share our favorite city the rest of the year. While trying to decide, I asked a friend whether she would be more likely to visit me if I moved to a coastal city in Mexico or Irving, Texas; the blank look told me what I needed to know.

During my months in Mexico, I have missed weekends in the mountains, birthdays, and going to concerts with American friends. I totally hate that, but not as much as I would hate basically walking out of those friends' lives forever by moving to, say, Conway, Arkansas.

Instead of relocating or retiring to a cheaper town in the U.S. and seeing current friends a few times a year (at most), a part-time expat life has enabled me to keep my life and the friendships I built in the American city I love. It's an option available to anyone struggling with the same type of choice.

"In order to live freely and happily, you must sacrifice boredom. It is not always such an easy sacrifice." - Richard Bach

Resources:

Expat forums are a great place to get very specific information about specific towns in Mexico (good realtors, areas to live, etc.)

Expat forums: Expatforum.com
               Blogexpat.com
               Expatexchange.com
               Expatfocus.com
               Expat-blog.com
               Yolisto.com
               Expatsblog.com

Checklist:

Hacks that help you make friends without talking much.

- Take the time to notice and acknowledge any changes; new hair style, a more upbeat attitude. People DO change and improve. Take note of it and make a comment.

- Keep notes on what's happening in the lives of people. Congratulate them on landmarks, a daughter graduating, a birthday for instance. You will find it takes no more than that before the person you are talking to will want to tell you all about it (you may not understand them in Mexico, but it buys you some time).

- An ice-breaker that I use at home and have just started doing in Mexico now that my Spanish is better is to ask a question, like, "I'm sorry to bother you, but I'm working on a [blog/project/article] and mulling over a question and asking everyone I meet their opinion regarding this one question..."

- If your Spanish isn't up for that, ask the definition of an *interesting* Spanish word you've seen. (YouTube Video commentaries can provide you with plenty of colloquialisms).

Most Mexicans love their language (and so they should!) and get enthusiastic about explaining more arcane words.

- Never go to a party empty-handed. If invited to a bigger event, bringing a high-quality bottle of tequila for a house gift is a good start. A bottle of tequila is received in Mexico the same way a nice bottle of wine is in the U.S. (They won't think you are an alcoholic. Mexicans *sip* their tequila). A recommended brand is Los Osuna Tequilas, which include the Blanco, Reposado, and Anejo tequilas. For a small event, a box of nicely-wrapped cookies will do.

- Mexicans reward graciousness. It is more looked down upon to be "*maleducado*," (impolite, inconsiderate) than to be financially unsuccessful. They are particularly sensitive to braggadocio (Spanish is rich in words for "self-entitled," "conceited" and "pompous").

- Mexicans have a different sense of personal space. If you go sit down in an isolated space of the beach, don't be surprised if an entire Mexican family comes over and sits down right beside you. Mexicans draw a circle around the group, rather than the individual.

- Anytime you invite a person out in Mexico, you typically are expected to pay the tab, at least until you have established a relationship.

- The most important phrase I ever learned about relationships, particularly those maintained at a distance, is "*You are what you share.*" When you are remote, try to share your experiences and photos more than you might otherwise. You cannot "over-communicate."

Chapter Three: Choosing Your Magic Carpet: Getting Around.

The bus that travels down the Malecón from my condo to my gym only passes by every twenty to thirty minutes. At times, that damn bus has flown right by me even while I clearly was waiting at a stop.

I guard against it passing me by standing out in the street. As it bears down on me, I wave my arms and yell in a manner impossible to ignore. The behavior is quite undignified but an hour is a long time to wait. It's the kind of Sturm and Drang that I'm glad no one at home has to see.

One evening at twilight, after reaching my home, I disembarked from the door closest to the conductor right in front of a young Mexican woman waiting to board. She gave an enviable whistle to get the driver's attention. In spite of that, the bus left her standing there. To my astonishment, with barely a glance at me, she shrugged her shoulders vaguely and began waiting for the next bus.

Buses in Mexico have taught me a great deal about myself. Most of it not good. They have also taught me quite a lot about Mexicans, traits that keep me coming back year after year.

For expats who do not want to deal with owning a car and driving in Mexico (and a myriad of reliable expat sources advise against it), buses make up the unavoidable third leg of their transportation tripod, the other two legs being Uber and cabs. Unlike the United States, where a good percentage of bus passengers are berserk, gesticulating wild men (like me in Mexico), Mexican buses are populated by the unfailingly polite and patient.

Mexican buses are usually privately owned, meaning that on the same route, you might get on one bus with televisions and recliners, and the next you will board and be transfixed by interior artwork depicting everything from Che Guevara to the ascending Madonna. The driver might be wearing shorts and flip flops as he muscles the gears for the frequent stops. These are the fastest and most entertaining rides.

At one point, late evening bus rides had become my favorite part of the day. Often the bus to my house north of the city was empty. I would sit in the passenger seat behind the driver, my eyes glued to the road with his, like my uncle's Irish setter used to do from the front passenger seat of his Ford Explorer back in Colorado.

One night, I stepped on a bus to hear to Madonna's "Material World" playing loudly through the bus driver's personal music player. I had never realized what a hard song it is to sit still to. What began as a little mutual head-bobbing ended up with the driver and I belting out the refrain, humming audibly to the same missed words. I thanked him as I boogied off, he grinned and waved before dashing off to his own nocturnal finish line.

A bus might wind its way through many parts of town before presenting itself to you. Poor, working class or more affluent people, all using it the same way you are. Riding with them will give you a quick survey of Mexican society. At times, a traveling entertainer will board with magic, a rap performance, or a song. They always give something in return for the pesos they receive from the passengers.

City *camiones* are not to be mistaken for the luxury buses run by private bus lines. Traveling on a luxury bus between cities is a comfortable way to go. Expats who own cars and would never dream of taking a bus in the U.S. take them instead of driving when in Mexico.

With the high price of gas in Mexico (4$ - 3$ dollars a liter) and toll roads being expensive in comparison to toll roads in the us, luxury buses can be cheaper than driving. They will even give you a sack lunch for the longer rides. You can find routes going almost anywhere, anytime.

I enjoy taking the bus to Mazatlán from the airport in Culiacán rather than going door to door like tourists do. As an example of how accessible the buses are, one can catch a bus between Culiacán and Mazatlán on the half hour all day and most of the night. The bus station has a dozen lines to choose from.

If you're thinking about traveling within Mexico while living there part time, ask local expats about the bus trips they have taken. The topic of bus trips is a good icebreaker and info expats love to share. Like European rail, I do not believe anything as comfortable as these buses exists in the United States (but then I wouldn't know, having been afraid to board a bus in the U.S. since 1975).

You probably do not need a car.

One of the earliest decisions you have to make when considering part-time expat life is what to do with your car at home. The costs of car ownership for the whole year to drive a car six months might make it untenable.

Studies have shown that private cars in the U.S. stand idle 95 percent of the time anyway. More and more in Denver I run into young people who think the whole concept of car ownership makes no sense, considering the escalating cost of insurance, taxes, payments (and that inevitable traffic-camera-ticket photo of you in dark sunglasses, furtively clutching the steering wheel as you stop just beyond the crosswalk).

For all the wonder of living in another country, especially one as populous and noisy as Mexico, it can be easy as a resident expat to begin to pull in, to retreat from the chaos. Owning a car in Mexico isolates you. Those who own cars often gradually move in that direction, year by year retiring more and more into the comfortable bubble of the internet, 130 television stations, and private dinners with a few close expat friends. I feel the pull myself at times, especially on those languid days in the summer. With a car, I could go on for weeks without talking face to face to a single Mexican.

Uber and car-Sharing services changed the game of being an expat.

Uber's arrival in Mexico certainly marked a watershed moment in my life there. For every time I bemoan not being able to jump into a car for a quick dash to the store in Mazatlán, I think of how much I've gotten out of my Uber riding experiences.

Uber is available in forty-five cities in Mexico at the time of this writing, up from thirty-seven cities less than a year ago. Now that Uber has made its way into smaller towns in America too, the idea of embarking on a part-time expat life is more viable than ever. Local competitors to Uber are also cropping up.

I usually sit in the front seat, like Mexican passengers do, to facilitate conversation. Their cars often have tiny front seats. At times on longer rides, I have to resist the urge to put my head on a companionable driver's shoulder. You are that close.

From friendly Uber drivers (which most are), you can find out where to buy a battery for your cell phone, where the largest garden shop in town is, and what Mexicans think of their president. I test conclusions about Mexican society with Uber drivers before taking my ideas to a broader audience.

When I remember to do it, I plan the topic ahead of time, looking up Spanish vocabulary to say things such as, "It's such a shame about the disappearing habitat of polar bears, don't you think?" and see where it goes from there. Often I bring up my favorite Spanish-language bands and eager-to-please drivers put music videos on their cell phone and attach it to the windshield for me to watch (and possibly to prevent me from going any further about the declining habitat for polar bears).

I frequently recruit Uber drivers for outside tasks. For 150 pesos, an Uber driver (an engineer) once checked the translation of a document I wrote in Spanish. I have paid them for a morning of errands for about 10$ an hour. I like that the cars don't display the Uber stickers on the windshield (they just flash their lights). That enables me to fantasize that I am riding with my Mexican son, nephew, or boyfriend.

Like almost everything else, Uber rides are cheaper in Mexico. Some people who have cars and infrequently use car sharing do not know that drivers rate you as a passenger just as you rate them. Tipping, how you pay (and bringing up the topic of Arctic wildlife) doesn't seem to make a difference in how they rate you in Mexico.

Mexican streets are vibrant, populous. Everyone has to make more trips out to accomplish daily household tasks. This can make for a real anthill. It is a good idea to text Uber drivers as soon as they accept your ride with clarifications (in Spanish) such as "The entrance is in front of the Palms Hotel" or "I'm wearing a blue dress (*Llevo un vestido azul*)." Make it easy for drivers to see you. Always ask, "*Dime mi nombre, por favor.* or *Como me llamas?*"(What is my name?) just like you have to in the U.S. Even Mexicans consider Uber safer than taxis.

Getting Around on My Worst Day in Mexico

I'm such a precise meal planner that after cooking the last meal of the week, I can find myself left with nothing more than a lime. One evening, feeling vulnerable and weepy, I forced myself nonetheless to go grocery shopping.

After lamenting listlessly how relentlessly unfair it was not to be able to go braless in baggy gym shorts to a major grocery store in Mexico, I crawled into a shapeless dress and called Uber. This night, my young, skinny driver (about four inches away from me) was uncharacteristically quiet, so I stayed silent as well. After about five minutes, I gently asked if he'd been busy that day.

He ventured into a conversation by saying he had two jobs. His primary job was doing maintenance for office buildings. Young as he was, he had three children, one he described as "mi sangre"(my blood) and two others.

I mentioned having some Mexican girlfriends and how lovely Mexican women are in general. The exhausted young husband assented, hesitantly paused, and then added furtively in a guilty confession, "Si...pero son cabronas!"

It was the first time I'd heard the word "cabron" in the feminine form, cabrona. The masculine form means a bastard, or a dick. I could not help but burst out laughing - the capacity for cabrona-ness being a trait widely shared among the sisterhood. I had a sense of what his day must have been like too.

At the grocery store, after a dazed half hour of forgetting why I was there, I made it to the checkout line. Crumpling my list into a ball, I did a basketball toss into the trash can behind the cash register. When I made the shot, I gave myself a celebratory thumbs-up (after all, it was the highlight of my day). No one had been paying attention except the elderly bagger, who saw how pleased I was with myself. We shared a moment, grinning at one another. He was still smiling when I left the store. So was I.

Leaving the supermarket, I couldn't bring myself to call Uber right in front of the cabbies who are parked in front of the store, so this time hailed a traditional cab to take me back to my apartment. As we unloaded the trunk back at my place, one of the condo building's maintenance men, a young, husky man who looks as American as any NFL player, rushed down the stairs to the cab, unloaded my bags into one of the building's wooden carts, brought the cart up the ramp, and then all the way to my twelfth-floor apartment. He unloaded the bags in my kitchen and refused any tip.

Would three moments of parallel grace ever happen at home in a single three-hour period? It's hard to tell. I am always struggling with whether Mexicans are so different or if I'm so different when I'm around them. Such experiences are not unusual in Mexico. Leaving the house feeling alone, even a few hours out in culture, being acknowledged in ways that do not seem to happen as much at home, will make you feel a part rather than apart from humanity.

If You Simply *Must* Have Your Own Car in Mexico

You may be unmoved by this story (however lovingly told) and conclude that having a car is non-negotiable. I can imagine that a single man would want to own a car, as would couples and those who enjoy the road trip from their country to Mexico. Driving, you don't have to worry about airline baggage limits, only how you report what you are carrying when you cross the border.

Many snowbirds make the drive to Mexico every year, even from Canada. I know of an older single woman who drives her mobile home from Alberta all the way to a Mazatlán trailer park on the beach every November. With few caveats, Mexico is safe to drive in. Ask Mexico Mike.

Mexico Mike, through his website and blog, has been an adviser to travelers in Mexico, those coming to Mexico to live permanently and those planning to be part-timers, for decades. His blog and website is the most comprehensive resource available on driving in Mexico. His website includes maps. He will even plan your trip for you.

According to Mike, you are allowed to drive in Mexico with your American plates with proper *Mexican* car insurance for up to 180 days at a time, matching what a tourist visa permits for your stay. If you drive a non-Mexican-plated car across the border but remain within the "Free Zone," which is a defined area within approximately twenty-two miles from the border, you do not need to apply for and obtain a temporary import permit (TIP) for your car or another vehicle.

The TIP is valid for the term of your original non-immigrant visa, or for 180 days from issuance. The TIP is no longer valid after that date, and the vehicle is not legal. In order to leave a U.S.-plated vehicle in Mexico and drive it on future visits, you need to apply for a Visa Temporal. A tourist on a regular tourist passport cannot leave the country without the car having a TIP. Outside that Free Zone area, all roads leading south have guarded checkpoints where cars without Mexican license plates have to purchase this temporary import permit.

Mexico has invested huge amounts of money to upgrade its interstate road network. Most of Mexico's new interstate roads are tolled. The toll roads are modern and well maintained, usually four-lane roads.

Expats with either a *visa temporal* or tourist visa can drive their cars into Mexico only with the proper documentation. A tourist may temporarily import his vehicle for a maximum of the -180day tourist permit. Even if you leave earlier than that, the vehicle must leave Mexico with the owner/importer. So obviously, you could not leave it behind for a future visit. Even if it quits running, you must remove it from Mexico. As long as your U.S. driver's license is current, it is accepted.

Buying a Car for Mexico

Some expats, after a few years, buy a car in Mexico. Then they realize that they have to find a place to store it while they are gone (Mexico doesn't have storage facilities for cars or personal goods). Next, they come to the conclusion that if they buy a vacation or second home in Mexico, they could store a car at their residence. All of which gives a great example of how cars can complicate your life.

One minute you need a car, the next you are buying a house in Mexico to have a place to store it. With this, committing yourself to all that home ownership entails, plus having to hire someone to watch over the house, upkeep of the car, and manage rentals while you are back home. Cars can make what was meant to be a simple expat life spiral out of control.

I admit that there are rare instances when I am not feeling so sociable and think longingly back to the polished black Nissan Rogue I gave up in 2014. So far, just when that longing begins to transform into a feeling of hardship, it is time to return to the United States, which temporarily distracts me from the lamentable fate of being chauffeured around Mexico by an army of young Mexican men.

Making Airline Flight Arrangements

If you intend to fly to your Mexican home rather than drive every year, there are considerations in making flight arrangements that are unique to longer stays. Rather than taking years to hone these skills, from the onset, consider two ideas: domestic Mexican carriers and airlines that charge little to nothing for flight changes. You will need to make flight changes frequently when you are a part-time expat.

Situations arise when you live in two countries that do not arise when making vacation flight arrangements. Your rental tenant in the U.S. changes his mind or his move-in date. A rental in Mexico you were counting on turns out to be thirty miles outside the city. You may want to change your return date for an emergency or a milestone birthday party.

At the very least, buy tickets directly from the airline. Ticket brokers like Travelocity do not make refunds. Or buy insurance that will cover you for flight changes. Fly Southwest or whatever airline charges the least for changes. Malleability in your flight arrangements will be important in your life as a part-time expat.

When you are considering how to get to and from Mexico, more creative options exist than expensive direct flights on American carriers. The San Diego/Tijuana airport at the border in particular offers a more adventurous option for those willing to brave the chaotic nature of traveling like a native.

The Tijuana airport has an indoor land bridge connecting to a building the U.S. side. From the U.S. side you can take an Uber or the shuttle to the San Diego airport to complete the domestic leg of your journey. I am aware that this sounds a little confusing —I myself had a illogically hard time wrapping my head around how to use the Cross Border Express the first time. From the Tijuana airport, you can take a cheaper flight to practically any larger city in Mexico.

The Mexican carrier Volaris is usually the least expensive of the Mexican airline carriers. When you are planning your biannual flights, go online to Mexican carriers and play around a little. Always check Volaris for any flights to and inside Mexico. Here's a sample of how much you can save, comparing the cheapest round trip flight from San Diego, California to Morelia, Mexico on Travelocity versus a flight from the Tijuana airport (20 minutes from the San Diego airport) to Morelia on Volaris, the Mexican carrier.

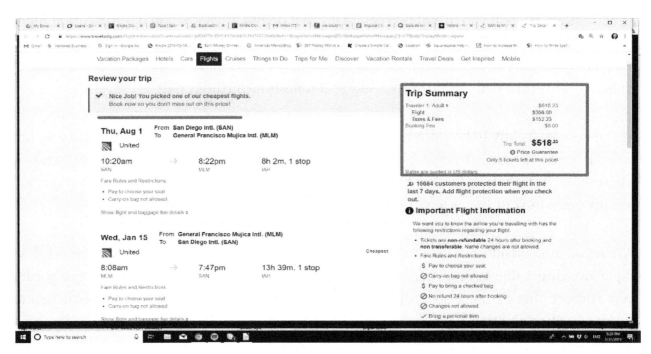

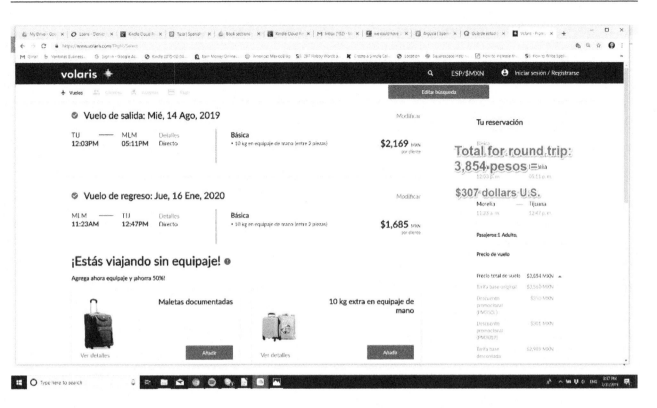

I have always saved at least a few hundred dollars on the round-trip ticket. I love the woolier nature of going this way, and all the little differences that make foreign carriers a fun way to travel.

Once you take the leap of flying domestic Mexican carriers, consider purchasing a pass for their VIP lounge with your ticket. The pass may cost 25$ dollars, totally worth the price in crowded Mexican airports with little seating and few charging ports for a laptop or phone. These kinds of indulgences, like using concierges and the occasional hotel stay, keep a little glamour in your touring rock star expat existence.

As much as I enjoy it once strapped in an airplane seat on Volaris, or peering out the window from a luxury bus in Mexico, I really don't like to travel. When hearing the word "travel," most people think of pleasure and fun. The word "travel" actually comes from the word "travail," which is defined in the dictionary as a "painful or laborious effort." Taking the word back to its Old French influences gets you "trepalium" (an instrument of torture), which gives the word the emotional dimensions I look for when trying to describe my own airport mishaps.

The second time I took the bus from Mazatlán to Culiacán, as the bus entered the city, it made a stop on the road before reaching the bus station. Thinking that perhaps the stop might be closer to the airport than riding all the way to the bus station, I asked my seatmate (definitely a Sinaloan as she wrapped herself in a blanket against the frigid -72degree bus temperature). She confirmed that indeed this stop was closer.

Flustered by the unexpectedness of getting off the bus, I looked anxiously out the window to make sure there were cabs. An open field lay out beyond the windows. Peeking out the door as it opened, I saw a row of taxis. With seconds to disembark, I gathered my suitcases from the hold and took a cab to the airport. Once arriving at the ticket counter at the Culiacán airport, I reached into my purse for my passport.

Hyperventilating grew into loud moaning, escalating into a full-on meltdown at the ticket counter as I realized I'd left my computer bag in the overhead baggage compartment on the bus. I didn't know if the passport was in the bag or not. The startled counter person at the airport offered to call resort personnel where I live in Mazatlán to request they check my condo for the passport. They also offered to call the bus station to see if they found the laptop bag.

I retired to the airport's seating area to sob.

An airport employee sat down next to my crumpled form and started a conversation. Jesús was an immigrant with a wife and child, who got deported from his home in Nebraska. Being from Oklahoma myself, we chuckled about the excitement of life on the Great Plains.

His immigration case made it all the way to the Nebraska Supreme Court. He won. However, the environment in the U.S was still too ambivalent for him to trust that he would not be picked up and put into a detention center anyway. He was waiting until he could be certain.

He asked if he could help me. In spite of the conversational reprieve, I was still so locked up in panic that I couldn't think straight. Leaving me in my heap, he corralled a taxi driver to take me to the bus station and escort me to its offices in the retrieval of my laptop bag.

I summoned up enough calm to make a barely-intelligible call in Spanish to an Uber driver in Mazatlán whom I had hired for errands. I asked what he would charge to drive three hours to Culiacán if my passport was found in my condo. I held my breath. He tallied up tolls and gas. He said reluctantly, 4,000 pesos (271$). (I can't imagine what it would cost at home to hire an Uber driver to drive three hours up and three hours back for such a mission).

The passport was not in the condo, leaving the computer bag as the only possibility (I don't carry my laptop in my computer bag, only paperwork). The cab driver (and likely former Indy driver) spoke on the phone with Jesús at intervals regarding our progress back to the airport.

Upon retrieving the laptop bag at the bus station, I found the passport inside. I checked my watch. Incredibly, I might still make my plane. The cab driver called Jesús back to tell him.

As we pulled up to the airport doors, Jesús walked out of sliding doors with my boarding pass already in his hand (How is that possible?).

They had closed the gate only minutes before. I missed the flight. There would be another flight in a few hours, the last one to Tijuana that day. The counter clerk told me it was fully booked. Jesús disappeared. Ten minutes later, the clerk reappeared. They'd make an exception and get me on.

I live in Mexico on the contents of one large and one small suitcase for months at a time. I was a few pounds over the weight limit for my bags. I couldn't think of a single thing I could discard without real sacrifice. I looked at Jesús beseechingly. He told me what I needed to do to avoid a baggage penalty (a process involving appearing like a homeless person in the lounge that I probably shouldn't share).

I returned to the U.S. from Mexico carrying only a few pesos. Jesús received no remuneration for his help, nor did he signal in any way that he expected it.

These are people we don't want in our country?

Embrace it as part of your expat experience.

All activities associated with getting from point A to point B as a part-time expat are pregnant with potential for drama; laughter, tears, relief, and comradery.

Years ago, I was a pretty good mountain biker, even winning a couple of races. While skillful, I still crashed into a lot of trees. As Keith Richards, in his excellent biography, *Life*, expressed after driving his car into a tree right in front of his mansion, "If you do travel around as fast as I do, you are going to crash into things." If you choose the part-time expat lifestyle, you're going to run into things too, just like the rest of us rock stars.

<u>Helpful Search Terms</u>

Mexican airline carriers

Best/worst airlines for flight changes

Temporary Vehicle Importation Permit (T.I.P) (if driving to Mexico)

Uber in Mexico/Car Sharing (local Mexican companies are entering the market)

How to travel to Mexico with pets/*Programa Mascota Viajero Frecuente* (for changes since this book's publication)

Best public transportation apps for Mexico (like Moovit)

Mexpro.com - for information on taking a car into Mexico

Resources:

Mexperience.com has a good guide for bringing cars to Mexico under the "Lifestyle" tab.

Mexicomike.com - is the most detailed resource on travel within Mexico.

You can read a thorough description about how to access the San Diego/Tijuana bridge and see a video of the route on my website Ventanas Mexico.com, *June 2018, "An Exhaustingly Thorough Guide to Navigating the Cross Border Express in San Diego."*

Checklist:

- Unlike in the United States, in Mexico you can change your payment setting to cash *(en efectivo)*. In a cash-driven country like Mexico, drivers prefer cash. They cannot tell which payment option you have chosen until they arrive. A few drivers are cheeky enough to call and ask if you are paying in cash after confirming the ride. They might even speed off while you're walking toward the car since at that point they know whether you are using a credit card. If arriving at your destination quickly is important, you should indicate on the settings that you are paying cash.

- Google maps: Touch the apps "Explore" icon, choose from the categories. The map's navigation and turn-by directions are on point and there are also detailed off-line maps so you don't use data.

- Public transit apps like Moovit work in Mexico and can be very useful in larger cities.

- The nicest buses may not be at the large municipal stations. Private bus lines usually have their own depots, with comfortable seating and a leisurely environment.

- The senior discount program (age 60 and up) in Mexico is called INAPAM. Information on the CURP card for senior discounts can be found at http://www.gob.mx/inapam. A *visa temporal* or resident visa is required to apply (free). One of the biggest advantages of having the CURP card is greatly reduced bus fares.

- In the U.S. most people begin by opening the Lyft or Uber app (Mexico does not have Lyft). There is a better way to do it. Open Google Maps. On the "Directions" tab, where you see options like driving, public transport, and walking, tap the ride-sharing icon:

the microscopic man holding up his tiny little arm. At that point, Google Maps shows you price and waiting-time comparisons between the two services.

- Contributors to expat forums all concur that if you decide you need a car in Mexico, buying it in Mexico makes the whole process easier.

- On toll roads in Mexico, emergency assistance is provided by *Angeles Verdes* (call 078).

- Save your receipts when using toll roads and buses as these will be needed if you are involved in an accident. Same for bus receipts - the ticket proves you were on the bus.

- Unlike U.S., restaurants are not common along highways. For long trips you should pack coolers and food.

- Renting a car in Mexico is expensive. Mexican law requires you have insurance to cover property damage and injuries to third parties. The minimum levels are $5,230 dollars and property damage of $2,640. This coverage is included in the rental price, as are all taxes and costs that are hidden in the U.S. Considering that you are driving in a foreign country, you might want to think twice about so little coverage when you could still be liable for much more. The most your credit card will cover is theft and collision. It is wise to have travel insurance as this will cover emergency medical care in the event of an accident.

- *If you give up owning a car in the U.S and want to rent long term while you are at home,* check aggregate services (like AutoSlash.com) and travel sites (like Expedia.com) that can check all rates at all the major rental companies at once. No one rental company can give you the best rates all the time. Check the contract carefully for hidden fees. Check to see if your credit card provides travel and car rental insurance as part of their terms of service. If you do not have such a card, apply for one, as they can save you hundreds of dollars on domestic car rentals.

Entering Mexico with a Pet

Plenty of expats and snowbirds come with their pets. To enter Mexico with a dog or cat (only dogs and cats are considered pets by Mexico; other animals have their own rules), you have to supply proof of vaccination against rabies at least fifteen days before arriving and indicate the date of vaccination and the date through which the vaccination is valid.

Pets need to be treated for internal and external parasites within six months of entering Mexico, as well as hepatitis and distemper. Treatment for ticks must be recent. Mexico accepts the three-year vaccine, the all-in-one vaccination is DHLPP for dogs. For cats, you should have both FVRCP-P as well as feline leukemia shots. The documentation has to indicate how they were treated, the manufacturer or name of the vaccine, as well as the vaccine's serial number. The requirements are specific, so make sure your vet on the U.S. side understands the requirements.

There are two options for documentation. With the first, each pet has the APHIS Form 7001 health certificate (HC) that has been issued and signed by a U.S.D.A. accredited veterinarian within ten days prior to entry into Mexico. A certification of good health should be attached or be part of the document. Mexico will reject VS Form 7001 health certificates if they are not signed by an accredited veterinarian and endorsed by a Veterinary Services veterinarian.

The alternative (and it certainly sounds easier) is that your veterinarian use a template for a certificate of good health, which is then printed on their letterhead that includes the accreditation number or photo of the license of the signing U.S.D.A-certified veterinarian.

The certificate must be issued within ten days of export. This certificate does not need to be endorsed by the U.S.D.A. No changes should be made to the wording in this document. The Health certificate cannot be handwritten. You also cannot use abbreviations for states, dates, or ages. You have to have the dog's name, age, sex, and breed as well as all the other testimonies of good health.

If you fly into Mexico often as a part-time expat, you might want to consider Mexico's Frequent Traveler Program for Pets *(Programa Mascota Viajero Frecuente)*, which streamlines the process of importing dogs and cats for frequent travelers.

Chapter Four: A Divining Rod - Having a Purpose in Mexico

They are the lost souls of Mexico. You see them wandering the streets disheveled, growling at the locals or catching happy hours at one o'clock in the afternoon on a Tuesday. They can be American, or German, or from practically any outside country. One world is made up of these expats. The other world is made up of expats who have a sense of purpose.

We are what we do. German philosopher Goethe said it with more feeling, "We are shaped by what we love." Having purpose changes your conversations. A sense of purpose puts you out in the world, engaging it. A sense of purpose makes us more selective about the information we consume and the people we spend time with. When you live a life informed by purpose, you enjoy your downtime more. You sleep better. You eat better. Living with purpose gives us a sense of peace.

In all the tasks involved with setting up a two-country lifestyle, as you think about your move to Mexico, you must contemplate your purpose while there. If you are in a phase of drift, think about how time in Mexico might help you find an anchor of meaning. The only unhappy expats I know in Mexico are those who, in the fervor of worrying about the logistical details, lost the binding ingredient of purpose.

Priorities change when there are fewer days ahead of you than behind, at least they did for me. To establish a career, you have to convince yourself you love the job, and perhaps the city it puts you in. Your success depends on projecting passion that cannot be faked. Once that imperative was removed, the fabric of my old ambitions was so threadbare, I couldn't mend it. Like it or not, at times we have to walk away, and trust that the instincts that brought us this far will not let us down, that we can begin again.

For a very long time—generations, in fact—we have known anecdotally that living in another country makes people more creative. Studies* have shown that living in another culture helps people make new associations and approach problems from different angles. Gestating ideas in a foreign country has a long tradition among writers, visual artists, and composers. Painters Gauguin and Picasso, and composers Handel, Stravinsky, and Schoenberg, created many of their most famous works in foreign countries, even when they were older. Nabokov wrote *Lolita* while living in Paris. Hemingway began writing *The Sun Also Rises* in Spain and finished it in Paris.

Many expats find themselves creating new identities, adopting lifestyles unlike any they have ever had before, or even thought of before. I know one living outside San Miguel de Allende off the grid, in the country. Nothing in the way she dresses, converses, or spends her day would give you any indication of how she spent the first 40 years of her life. If you read the forums and blogs, you see it's common.

Mexico is a country of fascinating incongruities that undoubtedly inspire people to express themselves in new ways. Once released from the confines of the past definitions they had given themselves, Mexico for many is a place of new beginnings.

The Myth of Passion and How to Find It.

What is your passion? It is easy to feel pressured to answer the question the way you always have, based on your past, not your future. It's okay not to answer that question, to even say for a period you don't have one. When a former passion no longer does anything for you, there's no reason to cling or feel guilty about it. Doing so only wastes time you could be spending searching for the street signs of new avenues.

My biggest regret when my old career imploded was spending five years trying to beat life back into it (continuing education, networking, interviewing) rather than letting go and using that time to find something new when I began to hate getting up in the morning.

One of the first signs that you are entering a new phase in your life is hearing yourself say, "I don't even know myself anymore." Disruption, chaos even, can be a useful and deliberate choice to make. "Cut short of the floundering and you've cut short the possible creative outcomes," wrote Denise Shekerjian in her book, *Uncommon Genius: How Great Ideas are Born.* "Cheat on the stumbling-about, and you've robbed yourself of the raw stuff that feeds the imagination."

According to Ms. Shekerjian's research, based on interviews with MacArthur Foundation grant recipients (the foundation supports creative solutions to the world's most urgent problems), being creative is a non-linear process, and periods of uncertainty usually precede an epiphany. We need to stay loose when we feel our creative well has run dry.

If past passions no longer motivate you, she advises, expect to flounder for a time. In computer jargon, you can compare this process to developing the code that directs one website (your old passion) to a new website (your new passion). You are rewriting your life's code, programming new ways of thinking to accommodate your new life.

What is the Best Way to Find a New Passion?

When I was thirty years old, I was introduced to mountain biking. While I can't say I hated it exactly at first, I sure didn't love it. But over the bruising, bloody months that followed, tiny successes, even riding over a curb, led to bigger ones and ultimately to scrims of single-track rimming rose-colored canyons in Moab, Utah, and weekends sharing the camaraderie of other mountain biking enthusiasts. I can say now that those were some of the most joyous moments in my life. Riding became a passion through engagement.

Similarly, I did not arrive in Mexico with a passion for Mexico any more than I'd had it for mountain-biking. My enthusiasm grew through engagement, particularly with the language and with the people. Seek engagement first and passion will often follow as you learn more and more, talk to enthusiasts, and actually participate, not just sightsee, however small in scale.

Some people credit the magic they feel in finding a new purpose to the universe calling. I credit it to commitment, to that moment when you decide you will do this new thing you've found, however meaningless it is to anyone else. I know one photographer whose purpose was to accumulate the biggest collection of photos of Mexican cantinas in existence. It took him all over Mexico. His portfolio is amazing. but more important is that he couldn't be happier. He is engaged in the world.

From the point of making a commitment, your life makes room for the changes necessary to accommodate it. Even changes that may seem negative - losing a lease, being dropped by a client, the end of a relationship - can open new doors. Rather than defeat, interpret them as green lights, and go. Once again on the move, looking ahead rather than behind and below, you will never want that feeling of giddy momentum to stop.

And by all means, go out and talk about your new purpose in life. That is a huge element of engagement (even if you have to do it in Spanish—my Mexican friends may not always understand why I am so excited but they do appreciate my enthusiasm.)

Start a new hobby.

The word "hobby" belittles how profound an impact they can have on our lives. Hobbies can shape our personalities. They can energize, inspire, and connect us with other like-minded people (online and in person). Most hobbies can be pursued just as easily in Mexico as at home. You can connect to enthusiasts everywhere online as well as in person and make the world your community.

The utter beauty of learning these days is the accessibility of online courses, books, YouTube videos, and podcasts to teach you anything under the sun, from anywhere, much of it free. Engagement in a hobby often leads to a larger sense of purpose.

In a survey of expats, these hobbies came up as to how they spent their days.

Learning Spanish	Sailing
Singing (groups in Mexico, church choirs)	Cycling
Playing an instrument	Yoga
Sewing, knitting, needlepoint, beading	Genealogy
Photography	Cooking
Jewelry making	Bird watching
Gardening	Sudoku
Pottery making	Art: drawing, painting, ceramics
Writing, journaling, blogging	Flea markets, garage sales
Hiking	Tai Chi
Flower arranging	Designing online courses
Scrapbooking	

To broaden the meaningfulness of a hobby to a larger sense of purpose, you must configure it in some way that deepens your relationships with others. Viktor E. Frankl, in his classic book, *Man's Search for Meaning,"* reminds us of what many religious instruct us – that the greatest meaning in life comes from the quality of our relationships.

Every hobby has a potential facet that can point you in contact with others and deepen your relationships. Most every Mexican town has charities and churches that are very welcoming of volunteers to plan events or teach English. Many expats find great satisfaction helping their host country.

An expat I know in Mazatlán started a quilting group where she teaches local women how to quilt. Another expat who loves building bicycles builds and repairs them for local kids. My own Spanish practices serve a practical purpose, but their deeper meaning comes from the relationships I have developed with my practice partners. Talking to them once a week for years now, I can these relationships are as authentic as many others I have.

One of them, Jorge Hernandez, a Mexican who lives in Querétaro, gave me his own take as a "local guy" observing expats who are what he sees as living life successfully versus those who do not. "Those who find groups to be a part of, a church or club, are the happiest. Everyone deep down wants to be a meaningful part of a meaningful group."

Expect some false starts.

Way too much emphasis is put on performance these days, causing people to retreat behind screens rather than take up a project that interests them for the sheer experience.

There's a sweet, pure joy in just doing and getting better. No one said you had to be a master at it. Not all engagement leads to dominance (I would like to say I had the same experience with my guitar lessons as my mountain biking...but, no.) Part of the fun is playing around, discovering.

Even activities that you try for a while will give you new insights, takeaways offering new associations that bleed into and invigorate the areas you know well—and a new appreciation of the subject (I for one will never look at blues guitar players on stage the same way as I used to).

You will have a more interesting answer to that question people cannot get enough of: "What are you *doing*?" That question will be as relevant in Mexico as it is at home. Even a few hours a day with a fresh purpose will help you again feel the wind in your hair.

Spiritual Journeys and Strange Days

One afternoon, my friend Estella and I went for a swim at a beach near my place and saw something that we still talk about to this day. Not even a hundred feet into the surf, we watched as a tall blond surfer threw himself sideways into the approaching funnel of water. The force of the wave would carry him somersaulting toward the beach. He would then leap up from where the wave carried him, and then go running toward the surf again.

He was a beautiful golden color, and wore board shorts. He had the classic surfer build; very broad in the shoulders and very narrow in the hips, his trunks barely hanging on. He ignored everything but the oncoming wave, motioning it with his hands as if saying, "Come on!" He never once looked toward shore.

Curious, I took my boogie board and swam out maybe 50 feet from him to get a better look. What I saw astonished me. His head was skull-like, his face lined and bony. His short blond hair was like waxed straw. While his body appeared smooth, at least from that distance, he was at least in his 60s, probably closer to 70 years old.

It was as if the head of a -70year-old man had been put on a -25year old's body. He continued to dive sideways into the approaching wave, and back-somersault toward the beach over and over, the kind of acrobatics I haven't been able to do since I was eight.

Estella had been watching him from shore too. From her angle, she'd only seen a young surfer doing a pretty amazing gymnastic routine. I told her the rest. Who is that guy, we asked ourselves out loud. She thought he might have been a famous surfer. I thought he might have been the devil - Notes from journal, August, 2017

Mexico is an authentically happy country. It is an authentically sad country. Mexicans learn to live with loss peacefully, not with the goal to "get over" it. Sorrow, when it comes, finds quiet acceptance here. No one tries to solve it. Our individual experiences become a part of the tapestry of a far greater human tragedy that Mexico is all too familiar with.

Mexican culture celebrates both darkness and light. Mexican poet Octavio Paz wrote in his book on Mexican culture, *The Labyrinth of Solitude,* "Our cult of death is also a cult of life, in the same way that love is a hunger for life and a longing for death." Duality.

Mexico, with its less materialistic and frenetic culture, offers an appealing backdrop for spiritual rekindling. I think it is safe to say that in Mexico, most expats have more solitary time than they did at home, more time to reflect. I have spent hours untangling my personal history in front of an ocean sunset, or inside a cathedral, hours for some reason I can never find in the U.S.

In Mexico, you have fewer superficial distractions. Life is simpler, which cuts much of the extraneous from your life, the dumb stuff, the annoying screeching of a society that cannot stand for you to look away for even for a minute. Mexico gives you the opportunity to feed that empty space, the space we all carry, it you just lean into it.

Expats who fail in Mexico, or are undone by her over time, are those who get their household routine established and have nowhere to go with their days from there. Introspection, meditation, prayer—all those activities that help you delve into your essential self are activities Mexico is made for.

In my first year in Mazatlán, I went into a day spa for a treatment. During the rub down, with my face down in that cushion - the one with the hole in it for you to breathe - to my utter surprise and embarrassment, I began to cry uncontrollably. Appalled, I bolted up and apologized, not having any idea what came over me. The aestician said not to worry, "it happens a lot."

We talked for a long time after that, whispering in Spanish in the darkened room about the nature of grief (She had lost her twenty-four-year-old son to kidney disease),and the crater it creates that's even bigger than the actual event. We discussed the benefit of meditation, and nodded over sorrows that never go away. I am certain that conversation would not have happened at home.

*Cultural borders and mental barriers: the relationship between living abroad and creativity. 2009, William W. Maddux INSEAD Adam D. Galinski

Resources:

"I don't want comfort. I want God, I want poetry, I want real danger, I want freedom, I want goodness. I want sin."— Aldous Huxley, *Brave New World*

Man's Search for Meaning by Viktor E. Frankl,

The Purpose Driven Life (Christian living) by Rick Warren

Life on Purpose: How Living for What Matters Most Changes Everything (behavioral-science based) by Victor J. Strecher

The Five Things We Can't Change and the Happiness We Find Embracing Them by David Richo (vaguely Buddhist influences)

Subliminal: How Your Unconscious Mind Rules Your Behavior by Leonard Mlodinow - While not billed as a book of finding your purpose, this bestseller will give you more confidence in the subconscious processes that are actually guiding your thinking and decision-making "behind the curtain" when you feel like you are being a bobble-head.

Chapter Five: Working Remotely from Mexico - Fact and Fantasy

In my home base of Denver, I have struck up chance conversations with a number of people, perhaps as they dragged their suitcases from Union Station or maybe getting on the 16th Street Mall ride and learned that they split their time working between cities or countries. According to the *New York Times*, over 4.8 million U.S. workers describe themselves as digital nomads. Eight million employees work remotely at least part time.

Over my time in Mexico, I have run into American geological engineers, graphic artists, trucking logistics personnel, and call center workers, along with artists, writers, photographers, and other creatives who take advantage of cheap airfare and the wide array of technological tools available to work remotely. Many are saving more of their paycheck even while having the adventure of their lives.

Unlike a digital nomad who has to continually be map-in-hand, looking for that next café with internet access and a decent room temperature, an expat who simply works remotely in an established second home. As an expat you can experience the culture in more depth, build close friendships and maintain a comfortable work routine. This "mini-life" comes fitted with deep relationships, favorite local haunts, and a level of intimacy you can't get just passing through.

When you take on this lifestyle, don't underestimate the power of the biannual voyage itself to stimulate your work with new ideas. The first few weeks of being back in either Mexico or the U.S. are my most productive times of the year. Everything feels brand new, whether I am walking the upscale streets of my favorite great American city or strolling the *malacón* in Mazatlán. Each is the same as I left it, yet each changes in subtle ways during each absence. Each time you make the crossing, you notice things for the first time that were there all along. A two-country lifestyle stretches your life's canvas. Mexico and the U.S. are perfectly paired for part-time expat life: What one culture lacks, the other will likely provide.

Having Your Own Gig

More people than you would probably imagine are earning their living from Mexico. Often no one, including their clients, know these people are not sitting at desks in Dallas or Chicago. Such is the power of good website design and a U.S. telephone number (one such financial planner working in San Miguel de Allende has a website landing page featuring the New York City skyline). We live in a world of infinite possibilities.

When I was first considering how to approach working in Mexico, certain specific tasks overwhelmed me. The thought of building a website and writing a business plan (both of which are helpful in distinguishing a business from a hobby in the eyes of the I.R.S.) stops many people in their tracks. Starting a business from another country has its own set of unique challenges, especially in the areas of communication and time management.

I found that by breaking the biggest tasks, such as putting together a website, into pieces, they were less overwhelming. Each large task was broken down into tasks that could be done in a few hours.

If a troubling piece stands in the way of your dream expat project, freelancers can fill in skill sets you cannot do or do not have the time to develop. A quick look through the contract professionals on sites like Fiverr, Upwork, Guru.com., and Freelancer will demonstrate how easy it is to fill certain skill gaps. I have hired graphic artists out of Australia, cover designers in Ethiopia, and my favorite, an Indian company that formats my books.

People might discourage you from hiring inexpensive foreign subcontractors from these sites, saying things like, "You get what you pay for." My experience with foreign subcontractors has been overwhelmingly positive. You might have to set a meeting in the middle of the night because of time zone differences. Language barriers require patience. All can be overcome.

These inconveniences are well worth it for the amount of money that can be saved. Formatting for my first book was quoted to me at several thousand dollars in the U.S. The Indian company I use charged 150$. While I am sure foreign freelancers don't always work out, you also haven't sunk in near as much to find that out. You can hire them to do anything. With them, there is literally nothing you cannot aspire to do.

The General Environment of Working Remotely

The world keeps getting better for remote work of all kinds. If you are still practicing a career you like and want to work from another country for U.S. dollars in a few years, *now* is the time to start positioning yourself. That takes time.

Almost thirty years ago, a colleague of mine asked our boss if he could work from home. I was shocked. No one had ever made that request in our company, as ours was an environment that required quick response time. He was granted the request. Why? Because he had spent four years positioning himself to make the request, demonstrating how responsive he was to team members and being a stellar on-site employee. Being a virtual employee is still a plum. Those who snag it have to constantly prove themselves even more than those with an office.

If a present job or employment is not conducive to remote work, start taking the steps to make yourself marketable to companies that do hire remote workers. Lists of such companies and positions are frequently published in magazines like *Forbes* and *Businessweek*.

Remote employees have to make sure they keep schedules, wifi strength, and time zones ever in mind, always adjusting to achieve optimal team productivity, rhythm, and flow. If you have not researched the subject of how to be a great remote employee yet, a treasure trove of websites promote products and services for the remote worker. All of them have useful blogs about how to increase productivity as a remote worker and adjust to working on your own

There are apps that will tell you when a client or colleague's time zone matches yours for scheduling meetings. Conferencing tools have gone way beyond Skype. Relationship-building apps and programs have been designed to build teamwork between people who will never meet face to face (they even have virtual running clubs and book clubs). In exchange for personal freedom as a remote employee, expect to work harder.

Employers who routinely hire remote workers have advanced tools to measure their employees' productivity, brutally objective tools that do not take into account soft skills. Employees who keep their jobs based on charm rather than production will not make it long in the new virtual workplace. Obviously, it takes a great deal of self-discipline. Without interaction in person, remote workers must "over-communicate" to colleagues and clients in order to maintain cohesiveness.

This might be completely different from what you were brought up with in your career. It certainly is different from my past work cultures, where no one wanted to hear from me unless I had a problem. Certainly no one wanted to read an email from me unless it was specific to him/her. That made my moving into a remote environment of online chit-chat and rules that required my response to every email having to be sent "copy all" practically impossible to get used to. I was hard-wired to a different kind of efficiency.

Additional Considerations of Remote Work from Mexico

You will not be very efficient at first in Mexico. As one expat friend described it, "Mexico is the perfect place for not getting anything done." In the ramp-up to making a living from another country, one has to factor in technology and other issues (like chaos) that you do not have to contend with when working remotely domestically. You will be hampered by the quality of internet service and other silly things like the lack of electrical outlets in public places for chargers and laptops.

In my last condo in Mexico, the internet went out every day at about 2:00 in the afternoon until around 4:00. When no one could fix the issue, it took a few weeks to reconfigure my work schedule and find other places to work online. I have spent entire mornings trying to find an inkjet cartridge or a *papeleria* (stationary store, where you will likely have to visit to find envelopes and paper).

Less availability of office supplies can turn what would be a two-minute online transaction in the U.S. into multiple trips to a variety of stores in Mexico. Stores keep very little in inventory. Multiple trips to accomplish the same task are the norm if you need something that cannot wait to be ordered online. Deduct 30-20 percent of your work time for these inefficiencies.

Paying Taxes on Income Earned in Mexico

As a contract U.S. employee or entrepreneur in Mexico, expats are allowed the same business deductions on their U.S. tax returns that they are allowed when working in the U.S. The cost of living in Mexico will be substantially lower, which should significantly offset any loss of income you might have while in getting started.

The I.R.S. does not expect a profit for the first two to three years of a new business. A good rule of thumb is to plan on not having income for at least the first six months, and as long as one year.

An expat has to pay Mexican taxes if the income comes from clients in Mexico. Examples of this would be teaching English or opening a restaurant or property management company, anything that the clientele are Mexican. If an expat is taking from the Mexican economy, they have to pay taxes there. Hire a tax professional, as how much time a worker spends in Mexico can also be a factor.

Workday rhythms are wonderfully different.

The daily rhythm of work life is different in Mexico. Mexico has a later work day schedule. They usually get started later and work until 7:00 or so at night. Computer technicians or accountants will make calls into the evening. People go out later and dine out later. You do not feel like you lost your whole evening because you worked until 8:00 at night. For me, this later schedule makes working late feel like less of a hardship (that and the ocean view).

Once working in Mexico, some expats limit themselves to a smaller world of English speakers and ignore much of what is outside that (very pleasant) bubble in order to complete their projects while here, and take more time off when in the U.S; others choose to get to know the culture. People can be happy with either. A bubble might be what you need at first. Isolation is great for creativity. My first year, I lived outside the city and had to take a bus even to get a cup of coffee. It totally worked for where I was in my project goals.

Working remotely from Mexico, your weekends can be filled with exploring a totally different country and language. Work breaks can be a walk on the beach or a stroll through a historical colonial district. Walking out into another culture and speaking another language while you are at it adds a whole new dimension to the words "coffee break."

Key Search Terms:

Best virtual jobs/remote jobs

Mail forwarding, virtual mailbox, mail scanning

Best companies for remote workers

Productivity tools for remote work

Best Freelancer sites (Fiverr, Freelancer, Guru, People Per Hour)

Team management apps, productivity apps, and team collaboration apps (such as Slack, Zoom, and Trello)

Apps for keeping time zones straight (www.timezone.com)

Checklist:

- You will need a U.S. home base to receive mail. If you do not have a trusted family member or friend who can receive your mail, you can forward it through filling out a form with the U.S. post office, or using a service like Traveling Mailbox or Earth Class mail. You can also hold your mail at the post office for at least a month (this seems to vary).

- You can make up some inefficiencies by hiring housekeepers and for home tasks you probably do yourself at home in the U.S.

- The IRS Tax Preparer Directory can help you find a tax preparer with credentials in preparing returns for remote workers and digital nomads.

- If possible, try out any freelancer for a less critical or urgent task first in order to test out language concerns, or hire them for a very finite piece of a larger project.

- Mexico is not a paperless society. In fact, you could say it is the opposite. You will need to show copies of all kinds of documentation for many transactions. If you live in a hot coastal area (as so many expats do) have these documents (rental agreements, proof of residency in an apartment, car registrations, and pet vaccination documentation) laminated at a *papeleria* (stationery store). Otherwise, they will disintegrate and be easy to lose.

- Uncle Sam is the jealous type (as if you couldn't tell). You have to file U.S. tax returns regardless of what country you live in the U.S. is one of the very few countries that insist on this). The general rule is that if you hold a United States passport, you have to file regardless of how many months a year you live in a foreign country.

Chapter Six: Staying Amused - Entertaining Yourself (and Others)

"So far, today has been a perfect day! I just returned from La Paz via the ferry this morning after taking four days to sail to La Paz, helping out a crew that is circumnavigating the planet …Sometimes I grab my surfboard and splash around the ocean. Sometimes I practice yoga in the mornings or wake up to the phone ringing, friends calling to make plans for the evening. I find that I am never alone when I venture out …Our up-and-coming theater directors, even if you don't speak Spanish, actors directed by their visions are understandable and entertaining." —T. Moore, describing his perfect day in Mexico.

"I wake up and it is a beautiful Mexican morning with the sun shining through thin clouds and a cool breeze ruffling leaves but not masking the sounds of chirping birds. Afternoon provides the option of listening to live music. All my friends are there and we dance with abandon. When there is a break in the music we catch up with each other, make plans for activities throughout the week and gaze at the gorgeous waves crashing on the sand beyond which are sailboats, parasailers and the islands." – M.H., writer, describing her ideal day in Mexico.

In your first months in Mexico, there will plenty new to see and do. These are halcyon days where life seems like an extended vacation. Yet, no matter how idyllic many days are, you will still have your frustrating ones.

Most likely the frustrating days will have to do with the language barrier. If, as they say, most disagreements we have with others stem from lack of communication (even when we share the same native language), it is a cinch that the statistic is not going to improve any when a second language is involved. I can go out in Mexico and the first three people I speak to will compliment me on my Spanish, only to have the fourth person indicate they cannot understand a word I'm saying. The following is a reenactment of a recent simple bakery errand:

> Me: *Por favor señorita, media docena de esas galletas [pointing to some wedding cookies in a bowl on the counter inches to my right].*
>
> Clerk: [Eyes widening as if a duck had walked in and started reciting the Mexican Constitution] *No hablo ingles!* (I don't speak English!)
>
> Me: [changing tactics, I point at the cookies and hold up six fingers] *Seis de esas galletas, por favor.*
>
> Clerk: [Still wide-eyed and shaking her head in utter bewilderment, she nudges her busy colleague at her side to see what she will make of the talking duck]

You can speak perfect Spanish and still, whether because of an American accent on your end or a closed attitude on theirs, at times natives in a host country will refuse to understand you when you speak their language, even when you get all the words right. My business partner, the Intrepid Elise, who is fluent in Spanish, including an admirable Mexican accent, still encounters this situation frequently after fifteen years in Mexico. It takes a listener time to switch gears from what they *expect* to hear from an obvious *gabacha*.

My Spaniard friends tell me, Iberian snobs that they are, that the better educated the Mexican, the better they will understand me if I am speaking proper Spanish. I have no idea if that's true or not. It does make me feel a little better

You will likely find yourself needing personal time to process these beleaguering episodes. Fortunately, less static in Mexico, and its fewer distractions, will yield you free time you never had before. Every expat I know has solitary activities to retreat here in paradise, whether it is photography, cooking, journaling, reading, or meditation..

The craving for more time to yourself will likely not be because you are lonely. In surveys of expats, living in another country appears to shift the psyche of the person abroad from that of being more "out there," to more "in here." They claim that this restorative reorientation creates a calmer, more distilled sense of self. As one American expat explained, before moving abroad she viewed herself as loud and outgoing. After three years living in Europe, she said the experience taught her to "take the backseat" more.

The Miracle of Music in All Its Forms

Maná, Alejandro Sanz, Soda Stereo, Miguel Bosé, Yuri, La Mala Rodriguez, Jesse Y Joy, Califanes, Enrique Iglesias and Gente Zona, Los Manitas Verdes, Juanes, La Ley, Babasónicos, León Larregui, Caloncho, Sofia Reyes, Mon Laferte, Jarabe de Palo, Duncan Dhu, Héroes del Silencio, Elefante, Hombres G, Jaguares, Maldita Vecindad, Los Prisioneros, Radio Futuro, Jaime Urrutia, Andrés Calamaro, Juan Gabriel, Jose Joaquin, Vicente Fernández, Silvestre Dangond, Luis Fonsi, Dudamel...

Remember the thrill of discovering new music as a teenager? It never occurred to me when I moved to Mexico that all those years I was listening to the Goo- Goo Dolls and the Red Hot Chili Peppers, Mexicans were listening to Maná and Soda Stereo, Spanish-language alt-rock, very similar to the music I love. The same can be said of any music genre. If you have explored most everything within your favorite sound palette at home, you can discover its parallel universe in Spanish-language songs and start exploring anew. Suddenly, a whole new universe opens to you.

If you are learning Spanish via Skype practice partners on sites like iTalki or My Language Exchange, music frequently comes up. It is a favorite topic of about half of my online Spanish practice partners. We exchange links to our favorite YouTube videos. We help one another with translating songs. Music lovers love sharing the joy that music has given them, and introducing foreigners to their old favorites.

Music unites. Countless Uber rides I have taken in Mexico have ended on a note of affinity after starting a conversation about a driver's favorite music (or asking him to explain Juan Gabriel). Familiarity with a few Spanish-language bands always surprises people and is a great icebreaker (as is the subject of Juan Gabriel). You can find live music all over Mexico, with detailed calendars published in online English-language news sites. These venues provide reliable places to find fellow expats and are usually free.

Surveys by the music industry show that most people stop finding new music after the age of thirty. Rekindling my interest by discovering new songs in my favorite genres provided many opportunities to connect in Mexico.

Even when you are barely aware of it in the background listening while you read or study, music can be surprisingly powerful. Research shows that music and certain types of background noise offer various cognitive benefits when it comes to factors such as productivity and creativity. Classical music and video-game soundtracks are recommended by experts as good types of music to listen to while you work. Music has a powerful ability to soothe, which you will need after an episode in your Mexican pharmacy or bank.

A Mexican friend of mine loves American country music. She doesn't know a word of English. She recognizes a quality in the singers' voices, similar to what she loves in Mexican regional music—heart. If you open your mind to the beats and sounds and ignore the words you don't understand, you can find music in Spanish that evokes in you the same feelings as your favorite American songs.

Learning lyrics to a few popular Spanish-language songs has enabled me to karaoke with appreciative Mexican teenagers on New Year's Eve and sing along with thousands of my Mexican sisters at a Yuri concert. Mexicans appreciate it when you acknowledge their musicians and Mexico's musical contributions. (From my own experience, I can say they certainly look at me differently when I belt out *"Muelle de San Blas."*)

Streaming Concerts – More Appealing When You Are Living in Another Country

Another activity you may never have done at home and should consider in Mexico is streaming U.S. concerts online. While I rarely feel the urge to do it when in Denver, participating in online streaming concerts holds great appeal when in Mexico as a way of staying connected to home.

You can stream live concerts for any type of music, including classical. Streaming concerts like the Austin City Limits Festival put on by Red Bull or music award shows like those run by HBO or YouTube (Coachella, Lollapalooza) can lift up a solitary night in a foreign country to a celebratory note.

You can leave the shows on in the background if you have work to do. Even pounding away on my website, it always moves my spirit up a notch. Sharing live-stream concerts with Mexican friends (and their young-adult children, which are often in tow) can be a bonding way to spend the evening (Mexican are much more used to listening to songs in another language than most of us are.

Television and Streaming Options in Mexico

In spite of all the ways we can call and talk face-to-face with our friends for free on apps such as Skype, WhatsApp, FaceTime (the FaceTime video/audio app is built into every iPhone, iPad, iPod touch, and Mac), streaming you can do the one area that you either sacrifice your money or your sanity in Mexico is media entertainment. Many are tempted to break the law as they have never been tempted before.

The situation of working around international movie and video licensing agreements turns sixty-year-olds who have never had a speeding ticket into unapologetic criminal masterminds. To get all of their movies in Mexico, many turn to Pirate Bay or Popcorn Time and illegal sources. [Note: Pirate Bay advises you get a VPN (Virtual Private Network, which hides your server location) before subscribing].

To a man or woman, all will say they would happily pay a fee, but they are not given that option. In some cases, it is either break the law or give up seeing the movie you are dying to see. Since many of us already feel like outlaws just by living in Mexico, it eventually begins to all make sense.

For another escape after a day of pantomime at your Mexican grocery store, no worries. Netflix is available in Mexico. The Mexican Netflix selection will not be the same as at home. People buy Netflix cards at convenience stores as well. They cost 150 pesos, about six dollars, for a month's viewing pleasure.

Netflix offers a wide range of high-quality movies and series in Spanish for those times when your level of ambition falls somewhere between studying Spanish verb tenses and re-watching Black Mirror. About 50 percent of the English-language movies have a subtitle feature for both audio and subtitles in Spanish. Not a bad way to mix pleasure with purpose.

Quiet evenings at home in Mexico can be just like quiet evenings at home in the U.S. Their best feature is that if they get too quiet, you can open your door and walk out into a completely different culture.

"What a perfectly horrible idea!...What time?"

One morning my Mexican friend Estella called, suggesting we go out for a glass of wine that evening. Well-oiled in turning down similar offers by friends in Denver who wanted to go to happy hour at five in the afternoon, I demurred. Late afternoon is a preposterous time to start drinking (unless you intend to keep drinking) that invariably leads to being dropped off at home at 7:00 p.m. just inebriated enough to be capable of little more than watching old YouTube videos.

Loath to turn down any gesture of friendship, I ventured to ask what time she was thinking about heading out. Estella responded that she'd pick me at around ten that night—as if "around" 10:00 p.m. was the most normal time in the world to begin the evening (which to me, it is—I'm just not used to anyone else thinking so too). I have seen this pattern repeated by all my Mexican friends (and of course The Intrepid Elise).

When I accidentally called an expat friend at two in the morning and she answered the phone as if expecting my call, I knew I'd found my people. Friends at home balk at any evening starting later than seven thirty. They are likely to flee the bar or event in mid-sentence if they look at their phones and it is past nine-thirty at night.

Due to work days that began early for many years, at home one has no choice but to fall in line with the 5-8 work schedule. The Mexican day runs a delightful two hours behind what we are used to at home as far as sleep and meal times. If you do not enthusiastically greet the dawn, you will find theirs a wonderfully sensible schedule for getting the most out of an evening.

In Mexico, I see ninety-year-old women propping themselves up in the corners of living rooms at 3:00 in the morning at family get-togethers. I see ten-year-olds running the streets at midnight on the weekends. If you are not a night person, learn to take a nap; otherwise, you will miss one of the best features of life in Mexico: its nightlife.

Try to avoid keeping rigid schedules that can be an obstacle to developing relationships in Mexico. Having a fixed daily schedule was one of the hardest habits to give up when I first moved. I had my list of to-dos and nothing could get in the way. My biggest social mistakes in Mexico often had to do with not wanting to deviate from my *plan*. I lost a few great opportunities I will never get back due to the inflexibility most of us bring with us from home.

As I've mentioned in my whiny blogs on the Ventanas Mexico website about friendships in the U.S. We treat friendships like work. We fit a quick coffee with our friends in between errands. We grouse over what we are going to do together rather than realizing that the time together, not the event, is what is important. By the time we reach 40, we haven't just hung-out with our friends without an agenda or a bar bill in years.

People Still Drop By

In Mexico, I've had different people drop by on the same day. Once six people knocked on my door at 10:00 at night. Don't get me wrong. I love it. I want to ply them with wine and inhale every single incomprehensible Spanish word they are saying. More daunting is that my callers, whether male or female, never fail to look less than stunning. I usually spend the first few minutes staring. The handbag goes perfectly with the jewelry. The stacked heels complement the romper. The starched dress shirt is worn as if it weren't 95 degrees outside.

Meanwhile, in the spirit of all things single and American female, I am wearing a tank top I haven't laundered since my arrival, denim shorts with a zipper that seems to open itself and thick dirty socks that I wear to protect my feet against the Mexican tile floors. Only one time was I lucky enough to be caught wearing work-out clothes that matched.

Mexico's Drinking Culture

Hopefully, you will be invited by a local to tag along to some of their music or dancing events. If drinking accompanies your nights out, know that the drinking culture in Mexico is different. According to the National Institute of Health, Americans and Mexicans are statistically intermediate drinkers (as compared to Europeans, who are the winners in the drinking competition category).

Yet, I have never seen my Mexican friends drink more than one drink, two at most, when out. I think Mexicans are more cautious about what, where, and how they drink. They love to be out. I have yet to see anyone out obviously drunk. When going out to even upscale bars, patrons most often order one signature cocktail, then switch to a final beer. They accept our American drinking culture with surprisingly good humor.

Mexican law has an altogether different, easier relationship with alcohol, without the draconian punishments put into place in the U.S. If you have ever had to leave a 20$ glass of wine on the table after deciding to leave a restaurant prematurely (say, because the waitstaff is ignoring you), and you are not driving, you know how maddening ABC laws in our country can be. Mexico's more relaxed attitude about alcohol will give you surprising moments.

On one occasion I invited my friend Lupita, to an outdoor concert with a big-name act. I was shocked to see drink prices on the flyer that listed "Tequila: 1,200 pesos" (about 40$ dollars), "Rum: 1,400 pesos," Seems a little high for a shot, right? In a moment of dissonance, I thought maybe drinks just cost that as such a big event.

As I sat in open-mouthed shock, the server clarified that individual drink prices were not even listed. Concert attendees purchased whole bottles and took what they didn't finish home with them.

You can go into restaurants in most parts of Mexico and ask for a beer to go. That is not to say Mexico does not have check-points and jails for detaining drunk drivers. They do. The legal limit for blood alcohol level is 08 in most areas, even lower in the states of Chihuahua, Jalisco, and Veracruz. These interdictions however, will not likely end your social life as you once knew it as they will in the U.S.

How Mexicans Write

Flaubert once wrote "Human speech is like a cracked kettle upon which we tap crude rhythms to make the bears dance."

At least that's true in English. Spanish dances flamboyantly. Mexicans are indisputably more expressive, even sensual in their daily writing and speech, and that takes some getting used to. Plus all cognates (words that are roughly the same in both Spanish and English) are not equal. Here is a ho-hum standard message from a friend regarding a trip she was planning for us to Durango, Mexico.

Hola como estas amiga bonita, te saludo y te comento que he estado viendo opciones para el viaje a Durango, te envié una página Viajes Dian. Vemos que conviene. Estare buscando mas opciones y te aviso si hay alguna otra recomendación. Recibe un fuerte abrazo. Me emociona una aventura juntas. TE QUIERO AMIGA!

Along with all the effort my friend is putting into the task on our behalf, the email starts with an affirmation of my beauty (which I thrive on), our friendship, and *saludos* which technically could be either hello or a salute (which isn't bad either). The message ends with a strong embrace and a declaration of love in capital letters.

This is basically how Mexican women write all the time. If that doesn't melt at least a little of your butter, you are dead inside. Of course it makes me insufferable with my American friends when I return to Denver ("where are my abrazos and besos?" I whine).

Other common words enhance the love fest in Mexico. The word "encantar,' which sounds to us like "to enchant" is used in Spanish to say you like anything from movies to hamburgers. You're likely to love hamburgers in the U.S. but in Mexico, they "enchant" you. ("Me encantan las hamburguesas!") "Tengo tanto deseos," sounds to us like "I have so many desires," but really just translates "I'd really like to…" But doesn't "desires" sound more passionate, doesn't it?

Whenever I was asked out on a date by a Mexican man, their mode of writing made me feel like they were characters from an Oscar Wilde book; it sounded so florid, I thought, until...

One morning I had Sunday brunch with a large group of accomplished Mexican women. I could barely understand the rapid-fire Spanish, but their eyes would soften in greetings redolent with endearments. Words like "cariño"(honey), "mi amor,"(my love), mi hija (my child), rose up into the air like softly popping soap bubbles throughout the morning.

Have parties early in the game.

Entertaining is nerve-racking at home. The road to becoming complete control-freaks is short once we graduate from college. We get so wrapped up in making the perfect impression that we miss the point. We want headcounts. We worry about perfect food preparation. We clean. In the U.S we are always upping the bar.

Mexicans never stop having parties. They typically spend a great portion of their lives at cousins' birthday parties, their nieces' *quinceañeras* and any of a number of other excuses to round the gang up *(Dia de Los Muertos,* Christmas *posadas,* and picnics in *el campo).* Given the sheer number of excuses they are willing to come up with to get together, if Mexicans prepared for all their parties the way Americans do, they would go broke and insane. You need not be so concerned with precision in planning parties in Mexico.

Once you've made a few Mexican acquaintances, tell your closest among them that you would like to host something. You can offer to host their book club, for example, or a family event, like celebrating a birthday. Set the time of the party as your friend suggests. You will have no idea who is coming. Mexicans are uncomfortable telling you no unless they know you well (in that case, listen for the Spanish word *hospital* (Mexicans do not mess around when it comes to excuses. If something is worth lying about, it's worth a *big* lie. I applaud that.)

In planning the start hour, for all that is written about Mexicans not being on time, it will not escape their attention that you are not Mexican. I have been roundly cuffed for tardiness in Mexico. By Mexicans. Plenty of Mexicans do not like the old tradition of being late, and some guests might surprise you.

While wine stores are common and wine is sold in grocery stores in Mexico, my own experience has been that you need far fewer bottles of wine when hosting a party there. Lighter drinks like wine coolers are popular with Mexican women. A bottle of very good tequila makes a good symbolic gesture, although rarely will a shot be taken.

Play a little music and be a good listener (since likely you will be helpless to do anything else, for vast swaths of conversation between *rapidisimo*-talking Mexicans). Every now and then, you might want to throw in "*más despacito, por favor,*" which will slow them down for a minute or two.

Don't worry if you have two people or twenty at your party. You are broadcasting a broader message. You are open for business. You are not an American recluse from the Mexican culture living in an expat bubble. Keep your expectations realistic. Sometimes the best bonding experiences are made up of only a few people. Be patient and soon you will develop an inner circle of Mexican friends.

Tickets to live theater, ballet, and concerts will cost anywhere from a third to a half of what they cost at home. Even if you do not speak Spanish, keep your eyes open for charity and cultural events to attend as another venue for meeting people. With or without Spanish, you will enjoy the performers' passion and interpretation of their art. If you find a gallery or museum opening, go, whether by yourself or with a friend. Mexicans who attend these cultural events have often traveled extensively, and a bigger percentage of people will speak some English.

Like in the U.S., cultural events attract people of good character who are engaged in their community. If self-conscious about your Spanish, inviting a potential Mexican friend to a concert or play will take the conversational pressure off. All you have to do is smile a lot, nod a lot, and be happy.

Friendships with fellow expats are easier to make than new friends at home in a new city. Expats huddle together no matter what country they live in. Your expat friends and you will share discoveries, insights, and funny anecdotes. Part of the fun of living in another culture is finding space in your brain to accommodate more than one way of looking at a situation. That is what living in another country gives you and your expat friends so much to talk about.

Typical evenings with expat friends largely involves bars and restaurants, maybe the beach if you live in a coastal area. (Disclaimer: perhaps not all expat cliques are the same. I can only talk about mine.) The most popular expat cities usually have periodic art walks or house tours. Expats get together to share Thanksgiving and the Fourth of July. They are visible to varying degrees depending on what city you are in.

Buckling up on the Volaris flight during return flights to Mexico, I always glance around at the good-humored, laughing Mexicans surrounding me on the flight and involuntarily let out an audible sigh of relief. My expat friends say that they do the same in their car when crossing the border by land. Like convicts who have stumbled across a prison door open, we frequently talk about relief we feel at that moment we go over the border ("You'll have to extradite me now, *cabrones*!").

Keywords for search

Live concerts for streaming

Free online courses (such as Udemy, Coursera, Lynda.com, Skillshare, Ted-ed)

Best music streaming (Spotify and its competitors in Mexico, Apple Music, Tidal, Deezer. Pandora is not available).

Best free movie streaming sites (We all know Amazon Prime, HBO, Hulu, and Netflix. You will be amazed by how many other free sites there are).

Checklist:

- Get a library card from your U.S. library, one that will enable you to download books from home while in Mexico. Most libraries lack extensive collections of books in English (exceptions: Guadalajara and Lake Chapala).

- Optimally, you will be coming to and from Mexico with no more than a few suitcases, making e-readers a necessity. E-readers can also serve as mini laptops, a backup should your laptop malfunction. A good portable sound speaker costs less than $100 and is well worth the weight in a suitcase – so much so you might even want to bring a spare.

- To get a regular network and CNN news, the most popular option here is a subscription to Canada's Shaw Network with a Shaw PVR (personal video recorder) receiver.

- Put some time into developing some music libraries and tools before leaving for Mexico. There are often technical glitches in Mexico, or downloads take longer.

- If you are not into podcasts now, reconsider them in Mexico. They are forms of entertainment that might be more attractive when living in another country. Overcast. com is one app to help people keep podcasts organized and facilitate listening.

- Want to go to a movie in Mexico? Local theaters play all the first-run movies. Most movies are in English with Spanish subtitles. American movies are typically subtitled in Spanish, rather than dubbed. The way to know is by the designation *dob* (dubbed) or *sub* (subtitled) designation. Tickets cost less, about 4$ dollars. You will not suffer.

- If you want to order a call brand, it is perfectly acceptable to ask the server to bring the bottle to pour in front of you, *"Hágame el favor de llevar la botella para verlo,"* or to ask for the liquor served on the side. I always do this and never had a single raised eyebrow.

- In resorts, particularly off-season when they are struggling for traffic, quality vodka might be substituted with an alcohol like Everclear, which you most likely have not seen since your freshman year in college. Although rare, some individuals experience the ir first allergic reaction they have ever had with grain alcohol. In these environments, always ask to see the bottle as it is poured.

- Continually ask yourself, "Am I set up to work or be entertained for two to three days without internet?" Always have a book or two downloaded into your hard drive, tablet, or Kindle. Keep a journal.

Chapter Seven: Technology

Tierra, trágame (Earth, swallow me.)

Meeting Bratty, First-World Technology Needs in Mexico

It had been the technological day from hell...again. Having woken up stoked about the work I was going to get accomplished, ah the excitement! Logging on to my laptop, a yellow exclamation mark told me once again I had no internet. What's more, the Windows 10 circle of death spun like a day of work going down a drain.

The building management, as well as my outside computer consultant, told me repeatedly that they'd "be there in an hour or so." After stewing all day in a broth of anger and frustration, at 11:00 at night, I went to the pool facing the beach to look at the water and ponder my fate as an author and blogger.

The security guard came over to tell me the pool area was closed and that I needed to leave. Given the amount of support I'd received from management that day, I told him I wasn't going anywhere."Me quedo," I told him defiantly. He nodded and left. Fifteen minutes later, the building manager approaches me and reasonably tells me he can't set individual rules for each person who lives and stays there.

I'd had a day. I told him if the building management wasn't going to keep its end of the bargain by having the internet it promised, I wasn't going to keep up my end either. He tells me he cannot control what happens on someone else's shift. He can only do his job on his own shift, which in this case was kicking me upstairs. He followed this with a very endearing description of his home and family life. Where it fit into the situation at hand, I wasn't sure, but it was making it frustratingly hard to maintain my anger as he walked me through it.

As tempting as it was to melt in the face of all this irrefutable logic and civility, I said that while I understood his position, I was staying right where I was. He said "Gracias" and left. Fifteen minutes later, the security guard returned, sat down on the wall with me, and said softly, without a trace of aggression or annoyance, brown eyes warm with compassion, "I understand you had internet problems today."

With such gentle interdiction (I would have been bludgeoned by now in the U.S.), I said that I understood such internet problems were a fact of life in Mexico, and perhaps not the fault of the staff, but that I needed to bleed off a little of the frustration of having wasted a day that started with such promise.

He said he understood and stood quietly a respectful fifty yards away while I gazed at the monochrome silver-and-black surf rolling in the darkness. Twenty minutes later, I rose and returned upstairs, vanquished yet again by the patience and kindness of the Mexican people.

If I never move to Mexico permanently, it will not be because of having to speak a different language, change my daily eating habits, or adjust to a radically different culture. It will be because whatever version of House of Cards that exists in 2023 kept freezing up in the middle of a stream. The only times I have been really angry at Mexico, and I mean swearing-like-an-Argentinian, has had to do with technology.

Each time you arrive to a country, whether to your home in the United States or to your place in Mexico, expect a collective cry from your electronics. If you listen closely, putting your ear right up against the device, the cry sounds a lot like, *"Where the hell am I?"* Some years my electronics have figured it out quickly, and issues like magic resolved themselves over a day or two. Other years, it has taken professional intervention, voodoo sacrifices, and a week or more.

One of my most horrifying memories of Mexico (other than my first trip to an open-air butcher shop) was when my Google searches began coming up in Spanish. In 2002, Google quietly changed it algorithms in such a way as to give search results based on your location (other search engines seem to do the same). Over time in Mexico, Google and other sites will come to believe you are Mexican, living your Mexican life.

Preempting technology problems, particularly by taking an extra laptop, is far superior to solving them in Mexico. Living in Mexico does make people better at troubleshooting, but if the keys on a keyboard go out, or the screen of a smartphone is dropped on one of the ceramic tiles that cover the floors of Mexico in its entirety, it is more of an issue than at home.

Having a laptop malfunction before technicians are lined up is an exercise in abject terror. One of the first items of business to take care of upon arrival to your destination Mexican city is to start looking for computer technicians to put on speed dial. That can take time. There are several challenges, finding ones who speak English, for example.

While it seems natural to try to find a fellow expat to help, you are better off with a young Mexican computer technician than an old expat one. Once the Mexican technician is safely in your door (and you have locked the door behind him), at least offer to cook him a five-course dinner. Sexual favors are not unheard of. Tip generously (which in Mexico means about 15$). Usually, the service charge will not be more than 300 pesos before tip.

Another reason to line technicians up early: technicians in Mexico tend to be more specialized. One might be the expert for internet problems, another for hardware or Windows issues. They travel to other cities and *pueblos*. They are in great demand, apparently enough to where they often do not need business cards, websites, or storefronts. Expats stalk them like wild turkeys in tall grass through referrals from other expats and through Mexicans and their extensive social/family networks. One cannot have too many in their directory.

When two keys went out on a practically new laptop, instead of the eleven-hour drive to the border for a new one, I got all excited about buying and using a separate Spanish keyboard instead (with tildes and accent marks! I enthused), until I discovered that the keyboard controls—capitalization, for example—are completely different on a Spanish keyboard (Amazon.com.mx has laptops. Oddly, you will find they too come with Spanish keyboards).

Nowadays, I carry extra chargers, e-readers, and telephones, as well as the extra laptop. These are the surprises that await you in Mexico. Technology might be the only blight on your metaphorical palm tree. Do not forget to bring a few decent set of headphones for when you are waiting in the coffee shop for the internet fairy.

Of all of these precautions, packing a spare laptop is the smartest move I ever incorporated into my trips. I have needed the spare for weeks at a time in three out of the first five years I worked in Mexico. The difference between waiting days for a technician when you have a spare laptop and when you do not have a spare is stark. With a back-up laptop, you might not make those inappropriate offers to Mexican service technicians over the phone. You can open the door to them when they finally arrive like a reasonably sane person. With a spare, you will not be hyperventilating as you call Jesús, César, and your housekeeper's nephew, trying the find the right technician for your particular problem.

The longer you are in Mexico, the more the Mexican YouTube channel will begin to surface in the place of U.S. YouTube, as will Amazon Mexico (that *is* what you wanted, isn't it?). After a few months, search engines get confused about your whereabouts. You can almost see the steam rising from your devices. Expect to have to figure out this redirection business on all of them.

Some expats move to Mexico because they really do not like search engines (or anyone else) tracking them. Mexico, even after all these years, still fosters a certain renegade attitude and outlaw mentality. This tendency, and believing you should have access to the services you are paying for makes VPNs particularly popular.

Virtual private networks (VPNs) are subscription-based services hide your server address. With a VPN, as long as you choose a server in the U.S., you will get the results you are accustomed to. (Note: once you've connected to the stream, you may have to turn the VPN off to prevent buffering. If you're blocked even with a VPN, try switching your browser.) The list of the best VPN services changes yearly. Hide My Ass, which has been around for years, is very easy to install and has good chat-box customer support (and unlike the others, you are unlikely to ever forget who your provider is). You will pay likely 12-7 a month.

I read widely varying reports on what VPNs can prevent blocking and what they cannot. You can only know for sure which websites will be blocked by trying to access them. Seeing the difference between having a VPN and not having one will be good for your overall understanding of what they are capable of specific to your interests.

Filtering searches according to where you are works in both directions. Switching server locations when you are in the U.S. can be quite enlightening too. When I in Denver and asked to look up the prices of certain medications in Mexico that are obscenely expensive in the United States, that information was completely unavailable. The few articles that came up in search on the subject were years old.

Once in Mexico and on local Mexican servers, I could look up what Mexican wholesale pharmacies charge for these drugs by doing a simple query in Spanish,"*Cuánto cuesta [name of the drug] en Mexico?*" With a VPN you can conduct research available in any country. You will see how much information you have been using U.S. servers and English-only inquiries only. America does not have all the answers. That is real power to any nerdy researcher on a project.

You will encounter electronic weirdness when operating in Mexico that defies explanation. Other issues in Mexico for me have been Windows bugs, charging problems, Bluetooth issues, Skype issues, and malware hacking operating systems. Sure, many of these issues could happen in the U.S. For some reason, however, they only happen when I am in Mexico. Every expat I know spends double the amount of time fixing technical glitches. This will improve your overall technical skills, which makes us all better people (or at least that's what I keep telling myself).

Internet reliability has increased a great deal in Mexico. Unfortunately, so has the surrounding population's reliance on it. Everyone has to adjust to more internet unavailability in Mexico. If the work you do has deadlines, count on it, and turn projects in a day or two in advance.

Rethinking Phone Contracts and Data Plans Before Moving to Mexico Part-Time

Consider your time frame for living in Mexico when choosing your next plan. If there is one thing living in Mexico will teach you, it is how Americans are gouged by the major carriers. At the very least, well before you leave, examine your carrier's Mexico plan (they all have them) before signing a new contract.

T Mobile has the longest track record of packages best-suited for part-time expats. AT&T is moving aggressively into Mexico. At the time of this writing, you can sign up for a $10/month plan that allows unlimited calls to and from the U.S. and Mexico and a gig of data. Customers can pay monthly, no contract, after the first two-month payment. (Once you sign up for the plan in Mexico, you stop by the AT&T office and pre-pay for the months you will be back in the U.S.)

Determined not to get locked into a contract, I bought a smartphone online and ported my old number on MagicJack, an internet-based service. Magic Jack gives you the ability to make and receive calls and texts to the U.S. for free (Of course service dependent on having internet service). In Mexico. Between these two services, my *total telephone bill is 25$ a month,* even after amortizing the purchase of a smartphone.

What are your data needs?

Google and Facebook both are moving into the territory traditionally covered by carriers. Some tools are free, others like Google FI, are not. How you choose comes down to your individual data needs, the all important question.

Generous data packages are still offered at reasonable prices in the U.S., and more than 95 percent of Americans remain under the most common packages available. When you leave your home country, data rates become more stingy. You cannot use the data for free. It is not uncommon for a carrier to charge 20$/MB (20,000$/GB!) as the default rate in another country, obviously not affordable to most.

Given the high amounts of data used routinely by many of us, this cost is prohibitively expensive for smartphone users. While it can be difficult to know exactly how much data will be used for a given action, it will be important to estimate your projected usage before selecting your tools.

To start, go to your phone's settings app. Tap on "Cellular," then scroll down to "Cellular Data Usage." You'll see your data usage (sending and receiving) over the cellular network for the current period, as well as call time in the section above it.

There are other ways to have internet access anywhere and not be limited to WiFi zones. You can purchase a mobile hotspot for about 150$ that will give you internet regardless of where you are. For those who cannot work offline for hours at a time, a reliable hotspot backup would be a necessity.

The point is not to sell you any particular solution (these suggested tools probably will be out of date before this book is even published) - but rather to demonstrate how you should research all the available internet options and phone plans, not just plans through major carriers but emerging internet based ones *both in the United States and Mexico* before signing any new contracts if you think you might be living in Mexico part time.

Data needs change with the expat life. Plan ahead and use tools from both countries and you likely will pay less on your communication needs than you do living in the U.S. full time. Ask other part-time expats and snowbirds with similar needs what they do. Time in Mexico is required to figure out what will work for your specific needs living in two countries.

Carlos, who handles the more mysterious internet problems for my building, had come again to the rescue. This time he brought someone with him, an outgoing, clean-cut guy about his age.

Thinking his companion was a trainee, while Carlos concentrated on my modem I asked him if he worked for Carlos. Oh no, he said, I have a fumigation business. We're just friends. We met through his wife."

"So you must be learning a lot about solving internet problems then, going on these calls with him?" I said, puzzled, "No," he said happily. "I'm not learning anything at all. We're just spending the day together."

Keywords

Best virtual private networks (VPNs)

Best mobile hotspots

Checklist:

- For short-term internet options, don't forget to check Telmex in Mexico. At the time of this writing, they had the option of a monthly contract for $1,311 pesos for the contract and $349 pesos per month. The contract could be canceled after two months.

- You are better off not scheduling any critical Skype meetings or calls for the first few days of a transition in either direction, while you help your electronics get over the shock of accompanying you as you fly like an untethered balloon over the continent.

- In Mexico and Europe, people have used WhatsApp, an internet-based service for decades. When you arrive you Mexico, your friends will expect you to communicate through WhatsApp. You can send videos, audio voice messages, videos and texts. All free (Although Facebook has purchased the company).

- Invest in extra *brand-name* chargers, as the ones for sale in Mexico are likely going to be after-market. "What type of charger are you using?" will be the first accusation a technician will make when you call. They will not do anything until you confirm the impeccable provenance of your charger. Carry a portable charger with you. As Mexico lacks the electrical outlets Americans are used to in coffee shops, airports, and public spaces.

- I have been told by several people that Macs (Apple) laptops are less glitchy when traveling.

- KeeptoGo - Reliable internet Sim card and a gig of data automatically, $118. Good support and you can take it with you in a car to access Google Maps. Not as fast a speed, 3G at best. If you are using the hotspot with your data, turn off the data-hogging software, like window updates and cloud backups, and absolutely turn off Dropbox because it will quickly gobble up your data. The service is metered, so you pay for the amount of data you use. Data is expensive, but you can pay for multiple gigs at a time for a cheaper rate. A gig of data is $45. Ten gigs $299. Pricey, but a backup. The system depends on cell phone signals so it works everywhere a cell phone does.

Chapter Eight: The Cognitive Dissonance Dance Club

In the States, coupling has evolved to the point that singles are practically engaged before they introduce companions to friends and families. I have close friends in the U.S. who have boyfriends I didn't meet until after they moved in together.

Before I go out on a first date in Mexico however, I parade the unsuspecting victim in front of my Mexican girlfriends for a read. It usually comes in the form of an ambush. I tell him to pick me up, then covertly arrange a house party for that same time. The few men who have ventured to ask me out do not even seem that surprised when a gaggle of Mexican women answer the door.

People introduce potential suitors early in the dance in Mexico. Even if I am no longer a naive sixteen-year-old, I don't think that broadcasting in a foreign country that you won't easily be culled from the herd is a bad idea (I like showing off that I even *have* friends). Now and then, I come across a chance article about a person disappearing in Mexico. I always ask, "Who were their *friends?*"

Standing in the crowd at a very well-attended open-air concert in the central plazuela one steamy August evening, I began talking to a handsome, well-dressed, and age-appropriate man from Guadalajara. He worked for Pemex and traveled to Mazatlán frequently for his job. His ex-wife is a doctor who decided her future was brighter in Los Angeles. We had a quick beer before he asked me out.

So as is my custom in these circumstances, I arranged a small pool party for the day that the handsome engineer suggested for our date. This time, I elected to tell the man first. He accepted the invitation and was comfortable with my friends. He brought a gift bottle of tequila, which I felt was very thoughtful. I placed it on the dining room table unopened. He seemed to enjoy the afternoon and left. After the party, I asked my Mexican friends what they thought. They were polite and noncommittal.

I've learned that with Mexicans, it's more what they don't say than what they do say. Finally one said, almost like an afterthought, that the bottle of tequila was of the poorest quality, something her husband would never drink.

Human communication is a miracle. Through the symbols of words, we are able to derive a universal idea and make sense of it. We are barely conscious of the hundreds of clues and innuendo woven into language that we can synthesize into a remarkably comprehensive impression after even a quick encounter with a stranger.

At home, we efficiently size up people by their work, dress, grammar, dentistry, the music they like, and the television shows they watch. We have environmental context in our favor and can draw on associations developed over a lifetime. At home we can tally up nuance and cultural markers as fast as we can speak. By the time we reach adulthood, we have developed such expertise that we can reasonably size up a person in less than thirty minutes, based loosely on commonalities and shared experiences. We name this ability "good judgment."

Now that you're in Mexico, throw all that out the window.

I am not a tequila drinker. I know nothing about tequila. I probably would have kept the gift bottle out as a display of generosity had it not been for my friend's comment. A 2$ truffle makes a better statement than a bottle of bad tequila. I missed the marker because I wasn't raised around tequila. My Mexican friends are not snobs by any means. They did not make tequila a topic of conversation. One person made one comment and they left the rest up to my awesome powers of reasoning.

In Mexico, you probably do not know what liking *banda* music says about a Mexican. Status symbols can be different too. Government employment in Mexico has higher status than in the U.S. Mexican men are often very close to their mothers by American standards. What should you think when one tells you that he goes to visit his grandmother *every* weekend?

When I researched Mexico before making my first trip, I would read the reviews posted for books, complaining that the advice given about Mexico was "common sense." Expats bray online about people arriving in Mexico and "checking their brains at the border." Both statements are unjust and unfair. How long had they been coming to Mexico before moving there? How much experience did they have with the country and culture previously? How much do they *really* remember about that first six months?

When you move to a foreign country, many comfortable social markers are missing and replaced with others (like tequila brands). It's easy to doubt yourself. Throw in the confusion of a second language and Americans' proclivity towards egalitarianism and it becomes easy to see how expats in Mexico get caught up in relationships with people they would not hang out with at home.

It is easy to think "maybe it's different here" when faced with puzzling behaviors. Expats and tourists easily find themselves giving behavioral license to friends or lovers in another country that they would not accept in their own country. You don't always know a cultural tic from an individual one. Even expats with years of experience in Mexico are challenged from time to time.

The Intrepid Elise had already lived in Mexico for thirteen years when we met. The training I received sharing that house on the beach near El Cid prevented me from making a lot of beginner mistakes, particularly money-related ones. Even she has her blind spots.

The Intrepid Elise had a rocking chair in the house that her grandmother had rocked her to sleep in when she was a baby. One evening, her Mexican boyfriend David, a white-collar professional who lives in Culiacán, leaned too far back in the chair and broke one of the rockers.

Even after all those years in Mexico, excellent Spanish, and as wide a circle of Mexican friends as expat ones, she leaped to attribute his indifference in repairing the chair to Mexico's culture. Mexicans, she explained to me, didn't care about possessions as Americans and Canadians do.

Intrigued by her assessment, I asked a few male Mexican friends their opinions. I received a curious array of responses, ranging from indignant (any real boyfriend would fix the chair) to acquiescence (what's a girl gonna do?). I am convinced that hundreds of expat are women taking *palapa* surveys all over Mexico right this very minute trying to determine whether the behavior of their Mexican husbands and boyfriends should be attributed to Carlos/Alejandro/César personally or blamed on Mexico.

We all want to believe that we have a value system which will guide our behavior accordingly and appropriately. When established values collide with new information, we experience emotional distress. I'd venture that most mistakes people make when they move to Mexico are not due to stupidity. They are due to cognitive dissonance.

Cognitive dissonance is defined as *the mental discomfort experienced by a person who simultaneously holds two or more contradictory beliefs, ideas, or values. The discomfort is triggered by a situation in which a belief, whether conscious or resting in the subliminal consciousness, clashes with new evidence perceived by that person.*

Elise justified her boyfriend's behavior as "cultural" because of his lack of concern rubbed counter to her belief of what makes up good manners. People want harmony in their beliefs. She restored her personal harmony by creating a cultural rationalization for behavior that went against what she considered proper, as informed by her Canadian upbringing.

According to behavioral scientists, the discomfort of cognitive dissonance propels the sufferer to resolve the conflict between a belief or value and new information by aligning it in one of three ways. We might seek more information to dispute the new idea (which is what I did by asking my male Mexican friends). We might de-emphasize the importance of the conflict, or we might change our belief (hardest to do since beliefs are often long-held).

Living in a different culture commonly surfaces conflicts between what you have always believed (maybe without ever verbalizing it) and what you see right in front of you. My first personal experience with cultural cognitive dissonance was less complicated than broken rocking chairs and more embarrassing: I found myself trusting people who spoke English more. Speaking English creates a halo effect. The unwarranted trust of anyone who speaks English (especially if wearing a polo shirt) is a common phenomenon among new expats.

The advantage of speaking English enables some Mexicans and your countrymen alike to take advantage of newcomers (see my essay on "Cost of Living"). Speaking English or dressing like an American obviously does not make one more honest, yet the relief you feel when you are being misunderstood and someone "saves" you with their English builds an instantaneous bond. Many expats doing business in Mexico could not be in business without this competitive advantage. They have a captive market of people who are afraid to do business with Mexicans.

One of the biggest con artists in Mazatlán is a sixty-plus- year-old realtor from Tennessee. Summer after summer, she rents out houses she owns that do not have hot water (who would check for that?). When I arrived, she seemed to be everywhere—everywhere expats were, at least. What appeared to be just another helpful, gregarious old expat was actually someone trolling her next American or Canadian victim.

A stranger's English proficiency in a foreign country can be like the branches covering over a pitfall trap, and not just a financial one. Just *enough* English (but not too much) can camouflage negative character traits for a long time, plenty long enough for a person to get into a relationship that would be awkward to extract themselves from.

Hence my argument for not making any important decisions or falling into any romantic relationships for the first year or two. I met several expats and English-speaking Mexicans with whom I felt an illogical emotional attachment in my first year in Mexico. Four years later, I look back and think, "What was *that* about?" The simple answer is the vulnerability of being new to a foreign country and a greater comfort level with people who spoke English. Once my Spanish and comfort level in Mexico improved, I saw some of these people very differently.

I had a similar experience about computer service when I first arrived. When you believe you hail from the center of the technical universe, it is easy to trespass into the assumption that technical talent is somehow *American* (I am willing to make this embarrassing admission in return for what I hope will be a teaching moment).

As a result of this prejudice on the parts of expats, American brethren whom I wouldn't trust with downloading Netflix onto my laptop hang up shingles as computer repairman. Expats go to them because it is comfortable rather than logical.

Having no technical vocabulary in Spanish with which to explain my needs kept me limited to whom I could hire, until I recognized what I was really fighting was my cultural bias. Learning Spanish helps you get past niggling little cultural prejudices that raise barriers and price tags.

After a period of a few years, I developed a full slate of Mexican computer technicians. I hired them by asking Mexicans for referrals on who the best computer specialists were, not whether the specialists could speak English.

As it turned out, all of them speak at least some English. The lesson gleaned from that is to *hunt for talent first and indeed, you are likely to get some English.* Americans typically are willing to pay more for services than Mexicans. Those who are good at their jobs are able to secure better-paying clients, Mexican and North Americans. Along the way, they pick up enough of the language to get by professionally.

The physical appearance of money represents another potential area of cognitive dissonance in Mexico. I always knew the exchange rate of pesos to dollars, yet there is something intoxicating about a pile of bills with "500" on them. I cannot imagine how I would have coped in Argentina during the currency crisis when it cost a million pesos to buy a loaf of bread.

Mexican landlords often ask for rent in cash. I would spread my rent out on a table feeling as if in the middle of a Mexican drug deal. Having to make three trips to an ATM to accumulate that much cash (due to the limit on the amount you can withdraw per trip) only exacerbated the frenzied illusion of illicitness, as did sorting and piling the bills by denomination on my bed, subconsciously expecting a police bust any minute.

Carrying it around again will revive your relationship with cash in ways not felt since you received an allowance. The incongruence between the number of bills I carried and the amount of money I had made me an unpredictable dinner companion. Several times I was short on the cash required for the evening because the stack of rainbow-colored bills I brought seemed like more money than it was. Mexico is still largely a cash country.

No matter how much my loose change in Mexico is worth, I still have a hard time leaving coins for a tip. The contradictory belief in the U.S. (or the cognitive dissonance) is the belief that it is tacky to give coins as a tip. Mexican servers love our helpless struggle with leaving change. I can't stop myself from leaving a 20-, 50-, or 100-peso-bill tips for a 40-peso bottle of beer. Neither can any expat I know.

Expats' favorite coin in Mexico is the gold ten-peso piece (about fifty cents). It has a nice heft for buses and tips. You can never have enough of these coins. Pesos will quickly accumulate in jars and the bottoms of purses. Your ten-peso coins will be gone in a day. A lovely coin.

The blue twenty-peso note exchanges to about a dollar. On the other end of the dissonance scale, I see tourists giving a twenty-peso note as a tip to a gifted street performance with obvious pride until someone finally points out that a dollar is not much of a tip anywhere, including Mexico. Or worse, I remember the confused, puzzled look of a little boy panhandling on the street, grabbing my hand, and showing me an American quarter he had been given.

Americans, including me, are always either under-tipping or tipping wildly, trying to get it straight. I'm proud to report that after a few years, most are so grateful to be in Mexico that they act like members the Bacchus Krewe in a Mardi Gras parade, delirious with their good fortune. Americans enjoy a reputation for being more generous than tourists and expats from *any* other country. Mexicans see the deliberate effort we make and the out-of-proportion guilt we feel when we screw it up. They take our flailing with the unfamiliar currency in convenience stores, cabs and *mercados* with remarkable equanimity.

Another area of cognitive dissonance in Mexico is the doctor's office. What you equate with high-quality healthcare (fancy offices, original art), and what better defines good care (good doctors) creates dissonance when you need medical care in Mexico. Doctors' offices here are sparse and utilitarian (wonderfully bereft of the cross-section picture of your internal organs. Doctors in Mexico are held in high regard by expats once they get past the cosmetics.

Even in how I dress I suffer from a type of sartorial cognitive dissonance. I'd never dream of wearing polyester in the States. Now it looks good to me. This is the most resistant cognitive dissonance I have. With every long-term stay in Mexico, my sense of what to wear in the U.S. deteriorates a little more. I have already been accused in Denver of dressing like Michael Jackson, my best attempt to date at becoming the stylish Mexican woman I really want to be.

All this confusion is actually good for you!

Studies of the plasticity of the adult brain show we have a much greater ability to learn in adulthood than we once thought, from learning new skills or knowledge to the capacity to change our social or political worldview. Educators deliberately incorporate cognitive dissonance in exercises to facilitate adult learning. Adult-learning theorists call it transformational learning—identifying and addressing our biases through action.

One study used foods that students believed to be "American" for an exercise in resolving cognitive conflict about what food constituted "a typical American diet" and the foods they associated with Americans of color. In the process, they learned of their biases and larger identities in their place in the world.

As an expat, you continually have opportunities to examine your biases in small, relatively painless ways. Step by step, you might even change your larger world view to a more forgiving and accepting one. Living in Mexico should be an exercise in personal growth. Personal growth is defined by therapists as being able to accept contradictory ideas and develop more flexibility in our thinking to accommodate new, perhaps even conflicting information. There is no better petri-dish for this kind of growth than living in another country.

Whenever you feel uncomfortable in Mexico, look at your belief systems and check for cognitive dissonance. Nine times out of ten, you will find the root of your anxiety crouching there. Recognizing and defining the cause of your unease is the most important step of resolving it, and restoring your sense of harmony with Mexico.

Checklist:

- Do not make any big decisions the first year coming to Mexico unless you know the culture well from previous experience.

- Keep and carry at least double the cash you normally carry at hand (or as an emergency fund) when in Mexico. You will not be used to how fast you run through cash if you are accustomed to using debit and credit cards. Smaller stores and merchants often cannot change larger (500-peso) notes.

- Whether it is in bills or coins, tipping in Mexico is 10 percent of the bill. You need to tip grocery baggers and those guys helping you park five-10 pesos too (and that twenty-peso bill is still only a dollar).

Chapter Nine: Money: How much does it cost?

The price of anything is the amount of life you exchange for it.

– Henry David Thoreau

The answer to the question of how much living in Mexico costs is more complicated than you might think. You could choose to pay the same 900$ a month rent in either country. The difference in the experience will be pretty drastic. In Mexico, you might be able to afford housekeeping services or cosmetic dentistry. You save money in the U.S. by not having any. Going out is far less expensive in Mexico, but you could *never* go out in the U.S. and save even more. If you attempt to exactly duplicate your life at home, you might save a little.

The cost of living in most American cities is rocketing. Retirees often move to less expensive towns, however now even younger residents are being forced out by the escalating costs. Half of my friends in Denver have had to leave in the last few years because of the rise in the cost of living. The great evolving political divide in America in between cities and the rest of America. If you are questioning your willingness to give up a stimulating city life and your likely hard-won relationships there, part-time expat life can enable you to keep your urban footprint.

In 2014, by moving to Mexico part-time, I cut thousands from my yearly budget. I have never felt the deprivation that the same budget cuts would have engendered had I made them living full time in the U.S. In fact, my life became several times more interesting and luxurious on half the money.

This arrangement with Mexico has enabled me to work with an ocean view six months a year and in Denver's trendy LODO district for the remainder of the time for less than 30,000$ a year. A -50,000$a-year life in a typical American city will costs about 30,000$ dividing it between the U.S. and Mexico. Considering what a -30,000$a-year life in an America city looks like these days, that matters.

Can a person live on social security alone in Mexico? The average person receiving a social security check receives 1,340$ per month. Perhaps you are sitting at home, wondering what life in Mexico will look like on that amount.

All is not lost. Let's look at that life positively and see what a retiree can do with that social security check and stretch their money. Instead of working until he drops, he could take that social security check of 1,340$ a month and live comfortably in Mexico. One can find a nice condo to rent, get some affordable health insurance, and still be able to go out with friends for dinner and a movie.

Many people who are terrified by the unrestrained greed of the healthcare industry consider Mexico. Estimates vary somewhat but a sixty-five-year-old couple on Medicare will need at least 345,000$, including Medicare Parts B and D for health-related expenses not covered by Medicare (according to Health View services, but similar estimates can be found from a variety of sources). This figure continues to rise. The average total saved by retirees (couples) is 374,000$, the median is 120,000$. Financial planners today blithely advise clients to "never retire" as casually as dietitians tell us we must eat five cups of vegetables every day to stay healthy. Never retire?

The Expat Solution

Technology has increased the accessibility of expat life and given us more options on how to shape it to order, whether you choose to work remote or retire earlier on less. Let's begin with some nuts and bolts.

A basic rule of thumb is that you can reduce your expenses by one third to one half for each month you live in Mexico. Here are some sample budgets for popular towns, representing both beach as well as inland lifestyles.

Puerto Vallarta

A beachside resort town that retains its colonial charm, Puerto Vallarta is known for its nightlife and resort-inspired activities. Its Old Town area is the focal point for both international tourism as well as popular among Mexican Nationals. (no Spanish required).

Resources:

www.soniadiaz.mx – a Mexican consultant with a very

informative website for expat information

www.pvmcitypaper.com – a local online newspaper

www.vallartalifestyles.com - Culture, entertainment and food

Chloe, single

Rent (more expensive area, on the beach or El Centro): $1,000

Lunch once a week in business district @$8 x 4 weeks = $32

Food: $450

Utilities: $57

Public transportation: $26

Transportation: Uber (once a week) = $25

Gym membership: $27

Internet: $22

Phone: $90 (U.S. international plan)

Streaming services (3-4) = $35

Entertainment (one movie, one live theater, and one dinner out per month): $90

Evening out with girlfriends, once a week: $20 x 4 = $100

Clothing: $70

Total: $2,024

Mérida (Yucatan peninsula)

One of Mexico's fastest-growing expat destinations. Beaches, Mayan ruins, inspired local cuisine, and excellent healthcare facilities (no Spanish required)

Resources:

www.yucalandia.com – Extremely well researched, covers the niggling and the big-picture cultural aspects of Mexico and the area

Two Expats from Mexico blog – Blogs are short and sweet with a focus on safety, consumer protection issues and language

theyucatantimes.com - Local English-language newspaper

Don and Barbara

Rent (expensive area, two bedroom) - $625

Food: $500 a month

Transportation: A gallon of gas costs around $3.50.
At two 15-gallon tanks a month: $420

Internet: $35

Phone: U.S. plan - $100

Entertainment: Dinner for two, full courses @ $32 twice a month: $65

+ 2 tickets to the movies twice a month @ $3.50 a ticket = $15

Clothing: - $50 a month (only Barbara goes shopping)

Utilities: $60

Housekeeping: @ $20 (two hours) twice a month $40

Miscellaneous: $100

Total: $2,010

Querétaro

Cooler mountain climate, Querétary is the best-educated city in Mexico and has all the vibrancy of a big university town (it has a number of universities and respected trade schools). It boasts a blossoming wine industry and the largest mall in Latin America. Excellent shopping and convenient to Mexico City. (For the most part, it is a Spanish-speaking city) It has a large international expat community, but remained largely undiscovered by Northamericans.

Rick and Miranda

Rent: $600 a month (three-bedroom) in El Centro

Mid-range dinner for two, three course: $27 once a week x 4 = $108

Taxi @ 72 pesos a ride/return every other day for a month: $60

Utilities: electric, heating, water, garbage, cooling: $30

Internet: $24

Fitness club: @ $34 each x 2 = $68

Food: $120 a week = $480

Clothing: @ $30 each x 2 = $60

Alcohol: $60

Entertaining at home: $100

Miscellaneous: $100

Total: $1,690

Puebla

Underrated by American expats, Puebla is an established weekend destination for Mexico City's elite. Cooler weather, phenomenal food, great shopping, and heavy influences from Spain (you will need to speak some Spanish here).

George and Henry, retired

Rent: 2-bedroom downtown: $450

Utilities: $15

Internet: $20

Basic meal in inexpensive (yet fabulous, because culinary arts schools graduate students to local restaurants), twice a week @ $4 a meal: $64

Food: @ $140 a week x 4 = $560

Transit pass @$11 x 2 = $22

George's daily cappuccino: @ 1.60 five times a week = $32

Taxi downtown once a week (about 5 miles) @ $6 a ride: $24

Clothes: @ $75 each (It's cooler there and they like to look sharp) = $150

Movie once a week @ $3 x 2 = $6 x 4 = $24

Miscellaneous: $100

Total: $1,461

San Miguel de Allende

The glow of Mexico's art mecca and wonderful weather has drawn expats and artists here since the end of World War II. San Miguel is an easy transition to Mexican life for retired expats and offers them lots to do; charitable events, classes, workshops, and tons of local fiestas to celebrate (no Spanish necessary).

Resources:

San Miguel Times (sanmigueltimes.com) - local newspaper

Trish

   Rent (expensive area): $1,050

   Utilities: $20

   Art supplies and classes: $100

   Internet: $19

   Lunch, including drink once a week in business district @ $7 x 4 = $28

   Flat Screen television: $700 (amortized) = $60

   Housekeeping: 2 hours every two weeks = $40

   Clothing: $75

   Gas @ $4 a gallon for economy car, two tanks a month for 12 gallon tank: $288

   Car insurance: $25

   Haircut or massage once a week $20 x 4 = $80

Gym membership downtown: $50

Miscellaneous: $100

Total: $1,935

Lake Chapala

Lake Chapala is an expat paradise with near-perfect weather and many activities to take advantage of it (golf, tennis, horseback riding). One can still immerse themselves in the Mexican culture here. A new road makes trips to nearby Guadalajara easy (no Spanish needed).

Resources:

Lake Chapala Reporter (local English -language newspaper).

The Guadalajara Reporter also covers Lake Chapala.

Joseph and Maria

   Rent: $700

   Groceries; $550

   Utilities: $35

   Internet: $30

   Netflix: $10

   Housekeeping (once a week @ $20): $80

Gardening: $80

Clothes: $50 x 2 = $100

Gas (two tanks a month), insurance and car registration: $350

Social activity budget for mix of movies, dinners, events: $140

Dental (cleanings/fillings): $50

Entertaining at home once a month: $70

Miscellaneous: $100

Total: $2,296

Hermosilla

Easy-going, safe and quiet, Hermosilla is located in the desert state of Sonora and a few hours' drive to beaches, mountains, and Arizona (Spanish very helpful).

Quinn and Emma

Rent (affluent area): $600

Utilities (heating, electricity and gas): $96

Internet: $23

Flat screen television (amortized): $40

Netflix: $10

Clothes: @50 x 2 = $100

Basic dinner for two, two days a week @7. a meal x 2 x 4 = $56

Drinks out, once a week for two: $8 a round = $16

Gym membership, @ $38 for two = $76

Quinn's haircut: $5, Emma's haircut: $15 = $35

Two tickets to the movies once a month: $6

Food: $600

Gas (two tanks a month) + car registration: $313.

Car insurance: $50

Miscellaneous: $100

Total: $2,121

Mazatlán

Home to 22,000 snowbirds every winter, major improvements were made to its malecón (the boardwalk running parallel to the beach) and central district in 2018. (The governor of the state at the time hails from Mazatlán and owns a number its hotels.) Mazatlán offers both beaches and a vibrant performing arts community radiating out from its Angéla Peralta opera house and community center (Spanish not required).

Resources:

www.mazmessenger.com - online newspaper

www.mazatlanlife.com – entertainment, arts and culture

www.vidamaz.com – expat newspaper

Sally, single

Rent: $900 a month (beachfront). El Centro would run about $600.

Food: $300 a month

Transportation: Uber (average one round-trip a day @ 45 pesos) $270

Internet: (included in rent)

Phone (Magic Jack and Mexico's AT&T) - $25 a month

Entertainment: $65 month (nice dinner and a drink three times a month)

Wine: @ 2 bottles a week - $70 a month

Clothing: $50 a month

Electric: $50 a month

Housekeeping: included with rent

Entertaining at home: $100

Miscellaneous. services: Netflix, online newspapers, Spotify premium: $25 a month

Total (living large): $1,805

Guadalajara

Mexico's second-largest city, a bee hive of vibrancy, near-perfect weather, and an economy a go-go. For the big-city person, this is the best choice, with all the convenience, nightlife and architecture of a big city without losing the charm of traditional *mercados* and *palazuelos*. It offers a good launching point for weekend trips and a much less chaotic airport than Mexico City (Spanish very helpful).

Resources:

www.discovergdl.com

www.the guadalajara reporter – expat news

Cesár, single

> Rent: (expensive area): $950
>
> Lunch in business district @$7 twice a month: $15
>
> Bottle of good red wine @ $13 a bottle, once a week: $52
>
> Food: $450
>
> Gas @ a tank a week $576 (Guadalajara has 8 million people and is spread out)
>
> Internet: $20
>
> Utilities: $54
>
> Phone plan: $40

Car insurance per month: $25

Housekeeping $5 an hour, 2 hours weekly: $40

An iPad (amortized): $46

Gym membership: $35

Flat screen television (amortized): $60

Clothing: $70 (César dates a lot. Guadalajara is a fashionable city.)

Drink date at an upscale downtown bar once a week @ $10 a date: $40

Expensive dinner for two: two times a week: $279 (César should get a girlfriend!)

Total: (living large): $2,752

Miscellaneous, interesting costs:

Cappuccino: $2.50

A gallon of milk: $1.60

2 lb. boneless, skinless chicken breasts: $4

1 lb tomatoes: $1.30

Monthly bus pass: $22

Mid-range bottle of wine: $8

Basic utilities (water, gas, electric, trash) bundled: $106

A new car, Volkswagen Golf: $16,000

A pair of leather shoes: $58

You might notice that prices in all the categories are pretty consistent throughout Mexico (this book doesn't cover Mexico City). You may see somewhat higher rental rates in pockets of San Miguel de Allende and Cabo San Lucas.

How to Choose a City

The city you are interested in may not have appeared here. Lists appear online frequently, by *International Living* in particular, ranking expats' favorite cities. Online research by name of city will yield their climate, proximity to airports, things to do, cuisine, size of expat population, history, and economy. A number of expats have written local guides on their city. The one thing they do not tell you is the most important element of all: The people environment.

We can read about attractions, regional food and Mexican art, but what ultimately breathes life into the expat existence are the people you encounter there. You will imagine the things you will see, but you will remember with more heat the daily chance encounters with the people there and the moments of grace they provide. Expat communities differ in their personalities. Some are cohesive (Lake Chapala, San Miguel de Allende, Mérida); in others expats seed themselves among the locals (Querétaro, Puebla, Guadalajara). Find your tribe first, then make that place your Mexican home.

The Desire for Less in a Less Materialistic Society

My journey to Mexico always begins with a domestic leg, a flight from Denver to San Diego. This particular flight was sold out. After a well-received remark on my great fortune in finding two slim, athletic people to sit between, I squeezed myself into the middle seat.

The guy on my left on the window-side was slight and sinewy. In the ensuing five minutes of light hearted small talk about how none of us were as in the shape we used to be after my remark, he mentioned being 43. He wore a baseball cap and a red sweatshirt. After about 20 minutes, he took the cuff of the sweatshirt jacket he wore over his tee-shirt and tucked the sweatshirt's cuff into the side of his baseball cap on my side, creating a kind of blinder between him and his seat companions.

He spent the rest of the three hour flight switching between email, and ads for a single pair of athletic socks and a particular 2,100$ bicycle, both of which he returned to to look at... over and over again, for the remainder of the three-hour flight.

The United States has the most sophisticated marketing expertise in the world Promotion is buried invisibly in the content of even respected magazines and newspapers (notably in the *Washington Post*). Much of the messaging is so sophisticated that we often don't register it at a conscious level, it's a constant subliminal buzz. At home, we are subjected to sales pitches while on hold on the phone, seated in cabs, pumping gas, and while waiting to see our doctor—all things you notice much more after you have spent extended time in a country where most of this still does not exist. Marketing never sleeps in the United States of America.

Interesting studies in urban planning indicate that city violence is greatly reduced when poor neighborhoods do not abut wealthy ones. We covet less what we do not see (according to Hannibal Lecter, who in spite of his flaws, knew human nature). During my first extended stay in Mexico, I was surprised by the sense of peace bestowed by not seeing, not wanting.

Occasionally, I do have to buy things in Mexico, usually gifts; wedding gifts, graduation gifts, or if I'm invited to a birthday party. These I purchase in regular department stores, the more high-end the better. I find that I have less confidence in Mexico in my gift buying. At home I can tell when an item from T.J. Maxx is practically identical to an item sold in Nordstrom. In Mexico I play it safe, making sure that the wrapping clearly indicates the gift's provenance. It's odd. My U.S friends have largely given up gift-giving, regardless of their financial circumstances. In Mexico, the custom remains very much alive.

No Refunds for You!

I once bought a pair of expensive pants at Guadalajara's *Palacio de Hierro,* the Neiman Marcus of Mexico. When I arrived home, I realized they were too large. I could not return them for a cash refund, only credit, which had to be applied to a purchase from the very same brand at the very same store, as explained to me by the gaggle of six attractive, near identical retail clerks all guarding the same register.

Much to the chagrin of expats and Mexicans alike, it is very hard to get a refund in Mexico. This applies to even the most upscale stores. Big chain outlets like Liverpool and Costco have the best return policies, but even those places will give you a hard time and be inconsistent in living up to their stated policies, offering you the convoluted conditions that need to be met in order to return a lampshade. Like in so many other ways, Mexico expects you to be responsible for yourself (I should have spent a few extra minutes with those pants before I bought them.)

Another reason you purchase less in Mexico is that Mexicans can fix anything. American consumers are wasteful, but often not by choice. We cannot get small appliances or electronics repaired anymore. Small carpentry jobs are not worth a laborer's time in the U.S.

In Mexico, I have had inexpensive side tables repaired ($28 dollars) and new locks put on bedroom doors of rental apartments ($50 dollars). Blenders do not do well with Nutella. I once paid $20 to get a new motor for a blender sacrificed in the interest of my sweet tooth. Spending $20 always better than spending $80 on such folly, plus I didn't add one more appliance to a landfill.

The implications of the arrival of Amazon in Mexico are still being sorted out. Generations of expats had to find "mules" to bring back electronics and real maple syrup (specifically Canadian maple syrup) from the motherland. Amazon still seems too good to be true. Expats are still too incredulous to order anything that costs over 20$. When I received an 8$ book I ordered just to see if I would receive it, the mail carrier was as surprised and delighted as I was.

Stocking Up on Mexico Before Coming Home

A month or so before returning home every year, I go into a near-hysterical flurry of attempted restoration: dental cleanings ($50), contact lenses ($50), dermatological treatments (plasma rich platelet therapy - $70 in Mexico versus at least $500 in the U.S.), and hair salon visits (a cut and hair coloring for $70 versus $200 in Denver). If I ever added them up, the money I save loading up on these services would probably cover a majority of my travel expenses.

Likely, some expensive elective medicines, prescriptions you live without but would make you either more comfortable or more attractive, can be purchased over the counter in Mexico at a fraction of the cost. For me, having discernible eyelashes makes life better. Lumigan, the same as the lash-growing "therapy" Latisse, can be purchased in pharmacy and without a prescription for 30$ versus 120$ plus the cost of a doctor's visit. A tube of Retin-A costs about 6$. Women are not the only expats making these rounds. My Mexican dermatologist has many male expat patients who say they'd never before considered such luxuries until they landed in Mexico.

Hiring People for Things You Hate to Do

Studies have shown that people are happier when they spend their money on buying their time back rather than buying tangible goods. This means that we are happier when we hire a person to do a task we don't like than we are spending the same amount of money on, say, a dinner out. Yet statistically people do not pay for these services. Why? The same studies indicate that people feel guilty about spending the money for a service. They believe people of character do it themselves.

Unlike the U.S., Mexico is a young country. It has a huge youthful labor force. Americans general willingness to pay a little more for services in Mexico than Mexicans do make Americans highly desirable clients. I found that if I am paying a person well beyond the local market rate for services such as housekeeping and the service still costs half of what it would at home, I am more likely to let go of my guilt - and be all the happier for it, just as the studies say.

Mexican hair stylists, masseuses, pedicurists, tattoo artists, almost any service provider, even doctors, are happy to make house calls. From time to time, we girls in Mazatlán get a few bottles of wine and have mani-pedi parties for around 25$ a person. It's a good afternoon for the manicurist, a good afternoon for us without any looming guilt. Everybody wins.

The Lighter Cost of Common Screw Ups

No expat completely escapes Mexican opportunism, which exists of course in every culture under different guises. In looking back on the years I've divided between Mexico and the U.S., in tallying up the number of times when I have screwed up, not done my homework and been taken advantage of, the total has been uncannily equal in both countries.

When I considered what these lapses cost me however, they have added up to more in dollars than in pesos. It is true that I once paid 20$ for a dollar's worth of *tamarindo* candy that I needed in my suitcase the next day. I likely have overpaid a host of Mexicans serving in a wide variety of capacities. But letting my guard down when dealing with U.S. telephone carriers, tenants, car dealerships, and even professional services such as C.P.A. has cost me far more. As a Mexican friend of mine who spent many years in Los Angeles put it, "Mexican scams are just poor copies of American ones."

At home, we are more likely to be gouged by a faceless corporation, which sanitizes the experience. It likely will not an indifferent global enterprise conning you in Mexico. It will be a real person looking you right in the eye and not flinching (when they sell you that tamarindo candy).

Fortunately. even your mistakes will cost less in Mexico, providing one of my favorite examples of ways Mexico saves you money that goes unrecognized by books on living in Mexico.

If you take Uber to a store in Mexico without checking the hours only to find it closed, that ride to and from that store might cost 20-15$ in the U.S. In Mexico, that same error would cost less than half that. Same goes for the bad meal you ate, the movie you did not like, and the disappointing haircut—all mistakes that happen sooner or later no matter where you live.

The lower financial penalty for error translates, for me, into taking more chances on entertainment. I might go to a movie wildly different from my norm because the ticket costs 5$, not 15$. I go to baseball games regardless of how interested I am in the teams because the ticket, nachos and beer costs less than 10$. As a person who hesitates ordering fancy signature cocktails rather than highballs in Denver, a big part of the freedom of living in Mexico has been not having to second-guess every small indulgence.

Learn Spanish for the Best Deals

Most of the same people who have made the fairly extreme choice of packing up their lives and moving to Mexico with a primary goal of saving money do not take the most important step to fully realize that objective: they do not learn the language. Many still think that most Mexicans speak English. Fluency in English, according to Mexican census information, runs between 5-12 percent of the population, depending on the size and affluence of the city (and your definition of fluency).

When I first moved to Mexico, I paid too much for haircuts. I could never seem to pull up the Spanish vocabulary for the visit. I would look up the words right before my appointment and then go blank when the stylist had the scissors to my hair. I paid more money to go to an American stylist because I was too lazy to fully memorize a half dozen words in Spanish. There are skillful, conscientious contractors and tradesmen who are far more reasonable in cost and will not work for people with whom they cannot communicate (fair enough).

Speaking Spanish is frequently cited by expats in forums as "the single thing I wish I'd done before I left." Putting all the other advantages of learning even some Spanish aside, like the friends you will make and control it will give you, if your primary aim is to save money by living in Mexico, make it a goal.

Checklist:

- If moving to a coastal area, think twice about any purchase of an expensive appliance or electronic equipment. Salt and humidity will destroy such items in short order - appliances usually only last a few years. Even the metal bits of my purses begin to show rust in less than a year.

- Price tags in Mexican stores tell you what they are supposed to tell you: how much you will be taking out of your wallet. Taxes are included in the price.

- When you are purchasing a service, the *only* way you find the best work at the best price is through personal referrals from people you know and trust. This goes for carpenters, car mechanics, electricians, plumbers, any tradesmen.

- The only way you know for sure the lowest going rate of many services is have Mexican friends who you can ask who have no vested interest either directly, or indirectly as a member of the industry in question. Harder to do than you might think as many service providers become your friends too...just like at home.

Chapter Ten: Renting Successfully...
The Crux of Successful Part-Time Expat Life

From my upstairs window, the house seems as if it is actually in the midst of the ocean. At times the surf hits the wall so hard it breaks three feet up the wall, then lands in the patio as if someone just threw a bucket of water on its floor. The house shakes with the impact. We never get tired of it.   —Journal, Oct. 10, 2014

The condo building has a large pool on one side of its back main entrance and a bricked patio area facing the ocean on the other. The Hotel El Cid's uniformed servers a few hundred yards up the beach will come over to our patio and good naturedly take our drink orders.   —Journal, Feb. 12, 2015

This place is the coziest of any I've ever rented. Decorated in peach tones and walls decorated with brightly painted geckos, it scores the highest with my Mexican friends with its semi private pool and ocean view. But what I'll always remember most about it will be its constant, gentle cacophony of sounds. At night, I can faintly hear revelers on the malecón at the foot of the hill. About an hour before dawn, I hear the birds shaking themselves awake. Then multitude of doves begins their cooing. By dawn, it's a beautifully balanced concert.   —Journal, July 2018

The U.S. Housing Crunch

Housing prices in the U.S have been rising faster than an author of a book like this one can keep up with. From 2011 to 2016, the median home price rose by 42 percent, compared to the median household income gain of only 17 percent.

The median rent for a one-bedroom apartment in Denver, for example, is $1,535, and closer to $1,800 a month in the better areas. The average home price is $530,000 and rising. In all but one of the fifty largest cities in the U.S., the income needed to pay an average rent or mortgage payment is higher than the median income.

Rising rents and the tight housing market in most major U.S. cities have become a serious financial challenge for many who cling to their dreams of the kind of life that only cities can grant*. I decided not to become yet another unwilling victim of the diaspora that flung friends to the far reaches of South Carolina, Central Virginia, and Arizona,

At times you have to be willing to give up something in order to keep it. In looking around me, I began noticing professionals with portable jobs spending months at a time in other cities or countries and renting their places "at home" out on Airbnb or through their social networks.

Even some semi-retired affluent couples in downtown Denver were doing it, renting their costly lofts out and spending a season each year in a different city or country. Could spending six months a year in Mexico save me enough money in those months to offset the higher cost of city life?

The Expat Solution

Before I began a two-country lifestyle, my life in Denver cost $ a ye50,000 a year. On that budget, life was still a bit of a struggle. Finally, I wrangled out a system that would allow me to live in an upscale apartment in one of the best neighborhoods in *U.S. News and World's Report's* best city of 2017 for six months and spend the remainder on beach in Mexico for less than 30,000$ a year. As mentioned in an earlier chapter (but is such a key point it bears repeating), living in two countries has improved my overall quality of life for half the cost of staying in the U.S. year-round. What it takes to do this successfully is what my books and the Ventanas Mexico website/blog are all about.

In the U.S. I savor convenience, familiarity, and personal relationships that took years to build. In Mexico, I realize the simplicity, graciousness, and personal revelations that come from living in a completely different culture. Part-time expat life opens two parallel universes, each pleasing in completely different yet complementary ways.

The crux of your part-time expat life, the key is finding people who will cover your rent while you are in Mexico. It makes no sense paying two rents (or a mortgage payment plus rent in Mexico) for the months you are there. As such, this is *the most important chapter in this book* (and assuredly the least entertaining) if you are seriously considering part-time expat life as part of a long-term financial plan.

Contract work, saving money to buy a home, or being new to a city are among the main reasons people look for six-month (or more) housing options. I have had inquiries from professional athletes looking to rent for their playing season. There will always be a shortage of reasonable options for such a tenant. Airbnb and their alternatives often lack privacy. Their daily rates are prohibitive for longer-term stays. Many hosts do not rent to the same person for over a month.

For the times you are off being an expat, if your current residence would not be marketable as a rental, then in the year or two ramping up for part-time expat life, you need to start looking for an apartment or home that is rentable. If you own a home, look at it objectively and determine what it would take to be attractive to a potential tenant.

Location, Location, Location—Smaller luxury apartments or condos in hip neighborhoods attract single, affluent professionals who are the perfect rental candidates. The smaller the place is, the easier it is to rent. Do your research. University areas attract graduate students and professors. Every city has its neighborhoods that newcomers gravitate to.

If your current apartment is located near one of those sweet spots, before you renew an existing lease, study it carefully to ensure that you can sublet, add a person to the lease, or make a similar arrangement before making any other plans for part-time expat life.

When an apartment complex doesn't allow sublets, there are still options. In my own state the Colorado housing code states that apartment buildings must allow two people per bedroom, including roommates. Check your state's housing code for a similar clause if your apartment complex does not allow subletting. It's a good idea to also review it to determine how enforceable such agreements are too, and what you have to do to enforce an agreement should a tenant or "roommate" default on payment.

Personally, I prefer taking apartments in large, corporate-run complexes. Corporate landlords play by the rules. At times, the rules are inconvenient; however, the companies can be counted on to obey rental laws and respect renters' rights (including your right to have a roommate, sublet, or whatever other rights are included in your state's housing code). Another advantage of corporate-run apartment complexes is that renters can usually set up an automatic withdrawal from their bank account for the rent, a clean way to set up the payment processes.

If you take a roommate for the months you are away, the roommate/lessee should fill out the same application you did when you signed your lease. You might have to pay a modest processing fee to your property management company, which you can ask your co-lessee to cover. Upon approval (by you and by the property management company), that person is added to your lease.

In reality, adding the person to your lease protects you as well as the property owners. With a lease application, you and whomever else is involved (owner, property manager) can do all the background checks necessary to secure responsible tenants. The property management company can also conduct checks and may have more access than you to certain information. For example, typically, they will require a social security number. Completely filled-out applications are standard for anyone being added to a lease making the process more formal and impersonal.

Another advantage with a completed application with their signature is that it gives you a contract in writing. You should also have your own separate letter confirming the dates, rent amount, and what is covered in the rent.

A formal application on file, whether it is provided by your property management company or using the template provided in this book standardizes the background information and makes it easy to check credit, work history, and references Completed forms make it easier to document why someone is turned down, which is especially helpful if you need to prove compliance with anti-discrimination laws in a sublet.

Choosing the right tenant is crucial to your peace of mind when you are in another country. A sample application form and checklist for screening rental applicants, including a "Red Flag" checklist, is provided in the resource section of the essay.

Here are the steps to renting out your place:

Pre-screen - Send interested candidates the application. Once they email it back, you can check references prior to meeting them, thus saving you that step if they do not check out.

Meeting in person - Have a half dozen questions ready, the most important ones being why they want to sublease, their income (their monthly income should be at least twice their rent amount), and "a little about themselves." Listen carefully.

Like it or not, we live in an age of transparency. It is the foundation upon which Airbnb and many other sharing services are built. If a potential tenant (or their sponsor, often a parent - I have rented to a number of interns whose parents are footing the bill) cannot convey what is going on in the potential tenant's life with a degree of transparency, wait for someone else. You need the story and it needs to make sense.

Be thorough in your background checks. Even if your property management company checks their personal and professional references and credit history, you should do it too. You have more at stake than they do. You are the primary leaseholder (and picked out the living room couch yourself). Check all past residences and employment, not just the most recent. Look for unexplained gaps in residence. Ask past landlords if they would rent to them again, if they got their deposit back, and how much their rent was.

Tip: Look for enthusiastic endorsements, not damp praise. Legally, our country makes it hard to evict a tenant. Believe it or not, people will give false good references to unload bad employees and bad tenants.

Oh, and about that chemistry? Ignore that. The more you like someone, the more you need to check references. I know that sounds counter-intuitive. Really hitting it off, or thinking you are hitting it off, with a prospect can cloud your thinking. Consider this: Over 50 percent of people surveyed say that it is okay to lie on a resumé. People can charm you when a desirable place to live is on the line. People lie. Even well-dressed, employed ones.

If you are considering a younger person, accept parents as personal references and talk to them. While I have never had to go to parents regarding overdue rent in Denver, I own a place at a ski resort in West Virginia where it is much more difficult to find stable tenants. Having the names of tenants' parents (and calling them when there was a problem) saved the day on more than one occasion.

Parents are oddly (and sometimes hilariously) honest about their children. You can get a real sense of how the person was brought up. Helpful information, that. Good parents, a good sign. Bad parents, a red flag (not a deal breaker of course, just proceed with caution. We do not lick our character off a rock).

Do not ignore professions. As much as we want to avoid stereotyping, certain professions do attract certain personality types and lifestyles. Do not think you can tell someone how to behave in your place. Find tenants for whom acceptable behavior comes naturally.

Do not rush. Make your flight arrangements for Mexico or wherever your expat destination is after you find the perfect room-mate/tenant. Build your travel schedule around their time frame. The caliber of tenant is more important than a month more or less in your second home in Mexico. All your scheduling should center on finding the perfect tenant first, and then arranging Mexico around that.

Bundle utilities and internet into the rent amount. You do not want to have to check with providers every month to make sure those bills have been paid. If you do not already have these bills paid automatically online, set them up to do so.

Your tenant should automatically transfer the amount (rent + estimated utilities + internet) into your checking account on the agreed-upon date. There are many services for transferring money directly beyond PayPal, including Zelle, Transferwise, or Venmo. They can also set up an automatic transfer on the same day every month through their bank with your account information (You likely will find yourself doing the same in Mexico.)

Keep a tastefully furnished, non-gender-specific apartment or home with a few creature comforts and a fully equipped kitchen. Look at Airbnb guidelines for hosts, and at the minimum follow those same standards. If something would make your place more attractive and cannot be trashed easily or is inexpensive, invest in it. Obviously, your place needs to be spotless when it is turned over. Appliances have to work. Towels and bedding need to be practically new. Quality furnishings, accent walls, comforters, and well-framed art will make your place stand out—and you want to feel like you are at home when you are there yourself!

Tip: Do not make assumptions about what would be useful to a tenant, such as your lawn chairs or bicycle. If in doubt, before turning the place over, have them take a look through the place and tell you what they want and what they would rather you store. Give them the entire space, with the possible exception of a locked owner's closet as long as that still gives them plenty of storage.

If you rent yourself, be a perfect tenant when you are in your U.S base. Show appreciation for your leasing personnel. Write good reviews on their web sites. If you are out of the country for half the year, you may need a favor someday. I find it useful to always be in the U.S. when the lease is up. If the rent has gone up, I take a little time to shop around and make sure I am still getting the best deal for my neighborhood.

Require an adequate deposit. Ask for *at least* the amount of two weeks' rent, which is nonrefundable if they move out before the agreed-upon date without *at least* thirty days' notice (the same policy as most apartment leases). Emphasize that you expect to be communicated with immediately should there be a problem. Communication is key. (I am clear on the point that if the rent is not paid on the date agreed upon, their deposit is used the next day to purchase my return ticket back.) Keep a full set of keys with you.

Ask for a nonrefundable deposit to hold the place and apply that to the security deposit when they move in. Make sure the tenant does not post-date a deposit check to the move-in date. Your bank will not accept a post-dated check, and the potential tenant can cancel a post-dated check anytime. It is worthless as a commitment. I recommend keeping the security deposit in a separate account (I use the membership account of a credit union). If you are living in Mexico part time, you should have accounts in two separate banks anyway.

If a potential tenant does not understand your logic and resists your security or any other deposit requirement, you do not want that person as a tenant. Do not apologize. Do not feel pressured or guilty. It's your stuff and your lease.

After you have left for Mexico, leave them alone. As long as the rent is being transferred into your account and you are not hearing from your property manager or neighbors, let them enjoy the place in peace as their own.

Think about recruiting a local presence. Sometimes it is a good idea to let the tenant know you have recruited people who can act as your proxy should a situation come up where you might be needed.

Let tenants know you want the place as clean on your return as you left it for them. Make sure to take pictures of the place as you left it. Provide them the name of a reliable cleaning service. Your return day from Mexico will probably be a long one. A big part of a successful part-time expat life is reducing the anxiety of certain parts of the process. Coming home to a dirty house or apartment makes you feel like a stranger in your own home. Cleaning services are worth it.

By setting up your expectations, they will probably do pretty well. Allow for normal wear and tear. Expect a dirty carpet, scuff marks, and some dinnerware chipped. Return the deposit within thirty days, after you have had a chance to run through inventory. Give back the entire deposit unless the damage is significant. Do not be petty or a curse will befall you.

Tip: Consider asking the tenant to leave their keys with a friend of yours when they "check out," a friend who can take a look at the place before you return. If the place is dirty, protect your psyche by having it cleaned before you get back (and deduct that amount from their deposit if the lack of cleanliness is substantial).

This is your home. It needs to feel that way *when you walk in,* not feel like an abandoned hotel suite. Build cleaning services into the rent if you must. Commit to spending it on that and only that, for whenever the need does arise.

Recently, I began the ritual of "smudging" my apartments upon arrival and departure. This ceremony is shared among a number of cultures, American Indian, Chinese, to purify a home of negative energy. The ritual, using prayer and the smoke from the burning of sacred herbs, was suggested by a friend (male, I may add) after I shared with him a number of strange happenings in my apartment.

I once jokingly mentioned to a new tenant (also male, an attorney) that I had performed the smudging ceremony before he moved in. He thanked me heartily and sincerely (I really do need to re-think my male stereotypes).

Maintain your U.S. place year round

Part-time expat life is much easier if you maintain your apartment or house in the United States extremely well in the months you are there. Do not wait until one month before you leave for Mexico to do the deep cleaning or to order the new dishware. You will have much more to do than you anticipated before you leave for Mexico. Quite a few of those things can only be done in the last forty-eight hours. Make upkeep an ongoing endeavor while at home, and save yourself a nervous breakdown when you are trying to leave the U.S. for Mexico.

Keeping your place in ready-to-rent condition year-round ultimately relieves you of being up all night on your knees scrubbing kitchen grout the night before your flight. Too many of those nights and you begin to dread the week before your departure the whole year. Do a little of the deep cleaning every weekend for the six weeks prior to your departure. These are the things you do periodically but not weekly, like washing windows, cleaning the insides of cabinets, cleaning moldings, and scrubbing that tile grout (Grrrrr).

A few days before you leave, you or a service can do the type of cleaning you probably do weekly, or that services routinely do. Keeping ahead of the cleaning will leave you with only a final wipe down the day before you leave when you will be wanting to say goodbye to friends and family.

Think about spending the night before you leave for Mexico with a friend in order to be in town the day the tenant moves in. You will get off on the right foot if you are available when they cannot find your internet code, rather than being on a plane to Mexico. Twenty-four hours staying with a friend before departure allows little things you forgot to do bubble up into consciousness while you may still have time to address them.

Storing Your Things: What, Where, and How

To turn your place into a tastefully furnished, non-gender-specific apartment or home ready to rent, you will have to store some of your personal things. When you have to pay to store them, you view them differently. I finally achieved my goal of a less cluttered life by being a part-time expat.

Have a discriminating friend take a look at what items or decorations you leave behind. Ask them to approach the job as if he/she were a tenant. We all have friends who can tell us if an item we love would be unappealing to a person not privy to its backstory. The beauty of the process is that when you return, you can get all those favorite personal things you keep back out and arrange them as if you never left. I can do it in a day.

After several years of screaming into outdoor intercoms in all types of weather and peering around blind corners for the homeless person who also had rented a storage unit, I decided to delete that biannual task from my life and hired a professional moving/storage company (Closet Box). I have been a happier person for it. You will be too (there are a few things in this book you have to blindly trust me on. This is one of them)

Moving and storage companies provide secure, bonded, temperature-controlled storage versus an unsupervised direct-key-entry storage unit you have to load and unload yourself. With storage pods, you must specify whether you want outside or inside storage if not storing it yourself.

Not only do companies that both move and store your possessions make your life easier, they also are cheaper than paying for movers and storage separately. To access your things, you simply make an appointment a few days ahead. They should have someone escorting you who will keep track of what is taken in and out.

Have boxes picked up for storage 2-3 days before you leave for Mexico. Live out of your suitcase those days. This gets them out of the way so you can finish cleaning, perhaps doing things like getting the carpets cleaned. You can see how it will look to your new tenant. Take pictures and keep them on file. Studies on the eye-witness accounts to crime demonstrates we all have far worse memories than we think.

Schlepping of boxes in and out of a storage unit is not something you (or your friends) will want to do every six months. The goal of part-time expat life is not to feel like a rootless vagabond. The goal is to feel like you have not one, but two homes you love. Moving your stuff to storage is an aspect of expat life not to pinch pennies on. Slogging back and forth from frequently depressing storage facilities will greatly detract from the whole feeling you should be going for with your expat life—that of international jet-setter rock star.

Simplify

There is a popular movement toward simplifying, ridding ourselves of things that do not create value in our lives. Nothing achieves this like part-time expat life. Over the years, I have come to look at my place in the U.S. as more of a *pied àterre* from which to maintain relationships, entertain, and be a place to come home to in the U.S. The fewer material goods you lord over (and I still have a few), the easier part-time expat life becomes.

As a part-time expat spending six months in each country, for 1-2 months a year I am simultaneously arranging to rent from someone in Mexico and to someone in the U.S. This mode of concurrently being a housing supplicant and purveyor used to make these stone cold sober weeks the most anxiety-provoking time of the year. It got easier as I developed relationships with people who were in on it.

This lifestyle attracts interest. People remember you and the idea. Your banker will remember your face when you stop by before leaving, the storage people when you call about the over-charge, the property manager who takes prospective tenant information for you, car rental people, all will remember you because yours is a life many dream of. With time and as

I developed contacts in Mexico, these months became no more work than planning a vacation - which in a sense, it is.

Renting in Mexico

> *The windows wrap around the corner, offering spectacular views of the ocean and the coastline. I've named it the "air-ium" because being on the twelfth floor, pelicans, paragliders, and willets fly by the window at eye level. The changing hues of blue of the ocean reach midway up your vision line*
>
> *—Journal, August 5, 2016*

Part of the fun of living in another country is exploring the different types of housing and neighborhoods available. Living in a neighborhood is the only way to know it intimately. None of my Mexican friends, natives to my city all, knew about the little ferry that takes people to the slice of beach near the marina that I love. I only knew about the little enclave because I had lived in a house up the street during my first year in Mexico.

As I detail in my book, *If I Onlh Had a Place*, about renting luxuriously in Mexico, stunning places can be had for half of what you likely pay to rent a decent apartment in most American cities. But you have to know the unspoken advantages that exist for expats renting in Mexico. Many are cultural differences you will never hear discussed by realtors.

At home, you walk into a leasing office, sign the papers, and rent an apartment. In Mexico, especially if you live there part time for months at a time, the best rentals are often uncovered by networking and through relationships. Most places are not advertised.

The places listed by realtors and even VRBO and Airbnb are the most expensive ways to go. Airbnb places in Mexico do not provide the scale of low-to-higher daily rates that one finds at home. They are never a "good deal," as people come to expect in Mexico. At best they are no better than a "fair" deal, and frequently very inflated to what Mexicans pay.

Here is the weird thing that happens with Airbnb in Mexico: Many American tourists come to Mexico and complain/remark that Mexicans assume Americans are "rich." Maybe that's true. And so do *expat American* Airbnb hosts. Although they live in a cheaper country, they charge the same or more than hosts in the U.S. Airbnb in Mexico is not nearly as evolved. There is much less of a range of options in Mexico than at home.

If you choose to use a realtor in Mexico, reputation is paramount. While Re-Max signs may be comforting, realtors in Mexico are not accountable to the same standards as in the U.S, nor do realtor professional associations enforce standards of ethics as they do at home. That is not to say there are not excellent realtors. I use one at times, and she is amazingly understanding of panic attacks, internet rants, and windows broken in the height of a tropical storm.

Using a realtor costs you more. People will write on forums, "Why not use a realtor? It's free! The landlord pays the fees." That's ludicrous. In that case, they simply adjust the rent upward. A rental rate may still seem like a pretty good deal when compared to rents at home, but it can never be as low as working directly with owners. The more time you spend there and invest in your relationships, the more personal referrals will surface.

The greater number of opportunities to rent fabulous places in Mexico by word-of-mouth spring from the same source as the pitfalls for either tenant or landlord of renting in Mexico:

Mexico's weak legal system. If that statement intrigues you, for more explanation, check out my book on renting in Mexico (otherwise this book would be at least 130 pages longer).

> *My condo building, in a restored hotel, boasted a grandiose marble foyer entrance, twenty-four-hour front-desk security, a cooled lap pool, and a gym. Coming home at night, the foyer frames our spectacular neon sunsets as if painted on an enormous canvas* —*Journal Oct. 2015*

Likely you will have to rent from an Airbnb, HomeAway, or VRBO-type website for your very first one-month stay. Play it safe for this trip. Unless you have friends in your chosen Mexican city and know the city well, you will not know enough to negotiate a particularly good deal. Consider it a cost of doing business until you know the market and develop contacts.

Follow your heart when choosing a neighborhood. Well-meaning expats, as they pummel you with where to find walnuts and what businesses takes CURP cards, will insist you need to live in the same neighborhood they live in, they "Can't imagine you living anywhere else." Areas under debate usually fall into two categories: gated expat suburbs vs. downtown historic areas (*el centro*).

When I was exploring my city, many tried to push me toward its historic area. I chose instead an apartment far from the action on a very quiet street to the north of town. It felt more comfortable to learn the ins and outs of the culture through strike-and-retreat, rather than embedding. If you are incubating an idea, a book, or a business plan, this type of isolation can get you there too.

Being a part-time expat allows you to experiment with neighborhoods for several months at a time, for years if you like. As you grow more comfortable in Mexico, you may be surprised which rentals become your favorites. What was best for Year One might be different for Year Three. By Year Five, I had learned to embrace the *banda* groups banging their instruments outside my windows on Saturday nights.

The House-Sitting Option.

Another option for renting a place in Mexico is to house-sit in your target Mexican town before deciding to rent there. Several single people do this in my town and seem very pleased with the arrangement. Homeowners will typically orient the house sitter to the area and introduce them to people who can be great contacts later should they ultimately decide to move to that city.

House Sitters watch over the place, usually take care of pets, and coordinate gardening, pool, and housekeeping personnel in return for a free place to stay. I recommend my friend Alex's website, Housesit Mexico, if house-sitting sounds like a good idea to you. Her service specializes in Mexico.

There are many more applicants than there are great properties. The trick to house-sitting is selling yourself. Produce a good video, look up the specifics about taking care of their particular dog breed, and use that information to give examples of your pet-care skills.

House-sitting is ideal for those who love animals (and can follow very specific instructions on their care), like quiet evenings at home (perhaps working from a laptop), and have decent handyman skills. You need to stay on the property most of the time. A bit of Spanish is needed for dealing with pool maintenance people, gardeners, and housekeepers. The cool part is that you live exactly how that resident lives, a great way to get a feel for everyday life in a particular location in Mexico.

In coastal areas, homeowners may leave for cooler climates during the hottest months and need a house-sitter for the hottest months. Before agreeing to house-sit, you need to be clear on what bills you will be responsible for, particularly air conditioning bills if the house is in a coastal area. If you house-sit, have your arrangement detailed in writing to avoid misunderstandings.

Establishing a reputation in the wise use of electricity makes you more attractive to any potential short-term landlords in coastal areas. I have first-hand experience in its exigencies. In my first stay, the Intrepid Elise followed me around in the kitchen like a shadow while I unloaded groceries to make sure I did not leave the refrigerator door open for even a minute. We hung our laundry on a line in the coastal humidity, where it dried stiff as a saltine cracker. This tutelage has paid for itself many times over in selling myself to potential landlords.

Which Brings Me to House-Mates

As scared as people are of house-mate arrangements, when I've been between places, at times the arrangement comes up and I usually view it as an opportunity to gauge just how weird I might be getting as a single person. Room-mates make great auditors.

Room-mates who already know Mexico are always good for at least a few laughs as you diplomatically attempt to ferret out critical information about Mexico, and these Mexicans who seem to be just about *everywhere*. I've always held the belief that the only way you ever know anyone is to live with them a while. It bonds you like nothing else. I'm willing to take a chance in return for that potential permanent bond.

I just made it into my room upstairs in the house I shared with The Intrepid Elise before the electrical storm began. Sheets of rain had begun to hammer the landscape in an angry alliance with the ocean just outside the window. On the other side of the patio wall the surf crashed, shooting up the wall and slamming down on the patio side. Lightning cracked through the palm tree grove in front of the house.

On my room's balcony, a plyboard appeared. Then above it, \a face. "I think I'm being electrocuted," whispered my housemate, wide blue eyes staring over the door-sized piece of lumber she gripped with one hand, hand drill in the other.

Glancing out the balcony, I could see the steel ladder she had used to muscle the three-by-five foot piece of plyboard up to the balcony as part of her annual preparation for hurricane season. I ran down the stairs and unplugged the bright orange cord.

*Water was everywhere, including pools on the balcony floor. "The funny thing about it," she explained later, "was that I've gotten **so Mexican** that I kept trying the drill, thinking I could stand the electrical shock long enough to get the job done."*

Pets

When I die, I want to come back as a dog in Colorado. Dogs get the best places by the fire in its ski lodge bars. They are fed organic food. They go wherever their masters (if you can still call us that) go. They appear, from their grins, to be clearly aware of their status as canine lottery winners.

Dogs have not ascended to this level of karma in Mexico. They have not gained a full-access pass in society like in the U.S., where any day now they will be given the right to vote (and likely will do it better than we do). When considering Mexico, you will be better off if you can find someone to board your pets while you find a place to rent and attempt to sweet talk your landlord into some kind of arrangement.

Resources: See Rental Application Samples at the end of this chapter.

Checklist:

- Some websites to consider in finding tenants (Google is always serving up new ones) are Sublet.com, craigslist, Facebook Marketplace, and Apartments.com. Use the screening methods outlined in this book. While people say many scams exist on craigslist, to date, I have found that almost all of my tenants on that site. The second most traffic has been from Facebook Marketplace. Sublet.com charges a fee on both ends to contact people. They charge the prospective tenant and the prospective landlord. So far, the website is too unwieldy, but check it - hopefully it will improve.

- When a tenant sets rent payments up with the bank, remind him that the transaction is a "money transfer," not a "bill payment"—do not let the bank terminology on some websites (like Bank of America) confuse your tenant. Always have enough in the bank to cover two months' rent.

- In decorating your apartment for subletting, lean toward the masculine. In the years I have rented/sublet my place, a vast majority of the prospects are male. Only one tenant has been a woman. For whatever it says about our culture, women can live with a slightly masculine décor far more easily that a man can live in a slightly feminine one (that means no white tables).

- Mexico does not have storage companies like the United States. You will not be able to store things in Mexico while you are away.

- Leases, as well as any contract in Mexico have to be in Spanish to be enforced

- Mexicans use air conditioning very differently from Americans. Mexico's electric companies give subsidies in the summer based on usage. If you go over a certain amount of usage (which American tourists often do), called *alto consumo*, they spank you with an electric bill that can be larger than a rent payment. The owner of the property may continue to have to pay the higher rate for a whole year. Dryers and refrigerators are the biggest wasters of electricity.

- Requiring "co-signers" is not a normal rental practice for expats. I would strongly resist any request for more than the first and last month's rent in advance. [my book, "If Only I Had a Place" covers these types of issues].

- Try to recruit a Mexican or a true expat local - a person who has lived there a long time and has Mexican roots or a Mexican spouse from the area – to help you look for your places. See if they will inquire about the rents for you without sharing for whom they are asking.

The place is on the 4th floor, close enough to the surf to see the individual waves as they crawl ashore, and close enough to see the details of each set. "I'm afraid your view up the beach to the north will be blocked by palm trees," the realtor had apologized. Yet every morning I lie mesmerized, transfixed by their gentle sway of their leaves outside the window right in front of me and the varying shades of silver the they take on their top surface side in certain types of sunshine and darkness. - Journal, August 2019

*Sources: https://www.census.gov/housing/hvs/files/

http://www.jchs.harvard.edu

Resources:

Closet Box Storage Ultimate Guide to Moving, Modified for Part-Time Expats

1. Label well

Always label your boxes on the side, not on the top. Since boxes get stacked on top of each other, this will ensure that anyone who moves your boxes can easily read the label (including you) if one day you need to retrieve just a box or two. Always keep in mind that someday you'll be unpacking these boxes. List contents in some detail. Don't forget to label boxes "fragile."

Use a magic marker to make arrows so the boxes won't be turned upside down.

2. Smaller is better

Think common lowest denominator of strength when considering boxes. Small and medium boxes are lighter and easier to negotiate up and down stairs. Keep weight to forty or so pounds.

4. Don't skimp on materials

At the end of the day, you're wasting your time and money if you skimp on packing materials.

6. Start early (four or five days ahead)

You might take a look around your house and think, "I don't have that much stuff. I got this. This will take no time to pack." You'll be kicking yourself when you're up all night before the movers come because you aren't finished packing yet. And likely that will be when you want to spend a little time saying goodbye to friends and family. It's the small, last things to pack, the ones that take longer than you realize to figure out how to pack, that will sabotage you.

7. Protecting artwork and picture frames

If you don't want to leave certain pieces of artwork on display when you rent your place, make your own boxes for paintings and picture frames for storage.

Wrap each item in bubble wrap first. Then use a flattened cardboard box to make a sleeve by taping one side shut. Slide your artwork into the sleeve, then tape up the remaining open end. Make sure to label your art box to ensure it's stored upright and moved carefully.

8. Televisions

Perhaps your tenant already has television. The best thing you can do to extend the life of yours is to pack it into a box. Either keep the box it came in or order a special TV packing box online. That will protect it while it's being moved around. With flat-screen TVs, you can break the pixels really easily.

9. Clothing

Make sure you wash and dry all clothing you are not taking before packing it away. For large amounts of clothing, store them in vacuum-sealed bags. Shoes (winter boots and the like) also need to be cleaned before storage Stuff each shoe with muslin cloth or another type of stiff fabric to help them hold their shape.

10. Bulky or awkwardly shaped items

When you're packing, you realize just how many awkwardly shaped items you own. Your best bet for storing or moving them is suitcases. "A suitcase with wheels is the perfect solution for these and heavy items," says Ross Sapir, president of Roadway Moving in New York.

11. Fragile items

Padding, padding, padding. Fragile items should be individually wrapped in bubble wrap or thick padding. Then, pack them tightly into boxes so they don't rub together, she says. You can also purchase boxes with built-in dividers, or snag some for free from your local liquor store. Other good places for boxes are big sports equipment stores like REI. Hit them up early in the morning.

Sample Rental Applications

Application to Rent

General Information

Date of Application

Full Name

Prefix   First Name   Last Name

Current Street Address

Street Address

Street Address Line 2

City   State / Province

Postal / Zip Code

Phone Number

Area Code Phone Number

E-mail

example@example.com

Social Security/US Visa Number

Birth Date

Vehicle Type/Make/ Year/Color

LICENSE PLATE NUMBER_____

Driver's License/Govern-ment Issued I.D.

Moving from

☐ Rental apartment ☐ Rental home ☐ Owned Home/Condo ☐ Family/Friend
☐ Other

Move-in Date

Lease length_____

Monthly Rent

Current Landlord's Name

Current Landlord's Phone Number

Area Code Phone Number

Number of Smokers (if any)

[   ]

Rental History

Previous Address

[   ]

Street Address

[   ]

Street Address Line 2

[   ][   ]

City   State / Province

[   ]   [   ]

Postal / Zip Code   Country

From

[   ][   ][   ]   📅

Month   Day   Year

To

[   ][   ][   ]   📅

Month   Day   Year

Previous Landlord Name

[   ][   ]

First Name   Last Name

Previous Landlord's Phone

[   ][   ]

Area Code Phone Number

or Email

[   ]

Previous Address

Street Address

Street Address Line 2

City State / Province

Postal / Zip Code Country

From

Month Day Year

To

Month Day Year

Previous Landlord Name

First Name Last Name

Previous Landlord's Phone

Area Code Phone Number

or Email

Present Employment

Employer

Industry

Phone Number

Area Code Phone Number

E-mail

Address

Street Address

Street Address Line 2

City   State / Province

Postal / Zip Code   Country

Occupation

Length of Employment

Current Salary

Frequency of payment

Additional Income Source

Liquidable Assets Source

Document proof_____

Liquidable Assets Source

Document proof_____

Total Monthly Income

Next of Kin\Emergency Contact

Full Name

First Name   Last Name

Relationship

Phone Number

Area Code Phone Number

E-mail

example@example.com

The Applicant consents to the collection, use and disclosure of the Applicant's personal information by the Landlord and/or agent of the Landlord, from time to time, for the purpose of determining the creditworthiness of the Applicant for the leasing, selling or financing of the premises or the real property, or making such other use of the personal information as the Landlord and/or agent of the Landlord deems appropriate.

By submitting this form, The Applicant represents that all statements made above are true and correct. The Applicant is hereby notified that a consumer report containing credit and/or personal information may be referred to in connection with this rental. The Applicant authorizes the verification of the information contained in this application and information obtained from personal references. This application is not a Rental or Lease Agreement. In the event that this application is not accepted, any deposit submitted by the Applicant shall be returned.

Submit

RED FLAG WARNINGS ON RENTAL PROSPECT SCREENINGS AND ACTION TO TAKE

	Is the application completed in full and legible	
	Does the signature on the form match the photo ID	
	Is the date of birth provided	
	Does the date of birth on the application match the date of birth on the photo ID	
	On the pay stubs verify that the name, SSN and salary matches what is on the application	
	Is Social Security number verified through a Social Security verification service	

Verification to Complete	
Has the Social Security Number on the application been checked agains a Social Security ID card, a legal tax document or a pay stub with the Social Security number on it	
Has current address on application been verified	
Does info on photo ID match information on application and the person applying	
Have you verified all employment and past landlord references	

LIFE'S SIX RULES
FOR SUCCESS:

1.- **TRUST** YOURSELF
2.- **BREAK** SOME RULES
3.- DON'T BE **AFRAID** TO **FAIL**
4.- **IGNORE** THE NAYSAYERS
5.- **WORK** LIKE HELL
6.- **GIVE** SOMETHING BACK

" JUST REMEMBER,
YOU CAN'T CLIMB THE
LADDER OF SUCCESS WITH
YOUR HANDS IN YOUR POCKETS "

Chapter Eleven: Staying Healthy for Your Rock-Star Life

Health Care Basics: Costs and Consequences

Once again, I find myself fumbling and sweating in front of a Mexican pharmacy counter, mugged by the full force of a coastal summer day, a day I began early knowing that anything having to do with a healthcare system anywhere in the world is likely to take up the majority of it. Fortunately, I don't think insomnia has killed anyone yet, not directly anyway.

The Valium, a stronger, more addictive second choice, was easy to get with my American prescription. The price quoted was 39$ dollars. After a few years in Mexico, you will learn that no matter what a medication costs, no matter how reasonable it sounds to your American ears, you always get a second quote. I declined the purchase, trudged up the street to another pharmacy, and bought the same bottle for 18$ dollars. But what I preferred was a pharmaceutical velvet glove to gently push me into my pillow, rather than deliver a knock-out punch.

To find a substitute meant running up still another street to a clinic, where, for 500 pesos (about 25$ dollars) where I could get a single month's supply of Lunesta - the velvet glove. A one-month prescription would mean making a return visit every month, in heat much like this, with the accompanying 500 pesos payment. I'm a wreck of matted hair and eyelids at half-mast. I cursed and gave them the 500 pesos.

Taking my case to The Intrepid Elise, I learned that there was one of those little doctor's offices, a consultorio, *right next to a gas station very near our house, which (as they usually are) alongside a Farmacia Similares, a chain of pharmacies that sell generic drugs.*

Within five minutes, the doctora, *made up like a Mexican telenovela starlet, gave me a three-month prescription for Xanax (Alprazolam). She charged me 100 pesos (5$ dollars). The pills cost 8$ dollars a month, and she gave me a six-month prescription. Satisfied that with three different sleep aids I would make it through the night, I went to Rico's cafe next door, worked, and swilled double espresso the rest of the day.*

For a person's first long-term stay in Mexico, being covered for health emergencies is the easiest thing in the world. Simply buy traveler's insurance *for health emergencies only* which is much cheaper. According to Monica Paxon, author of *The English Speaker's Guide to Health Care in Mexico,* before you come to Mexico, if you have any ongoing health needs, you should have your medical records translated into Spanish. Put the documents, including drug names, on a flash drive and bring them with you, along with contact information for your insurance company.

A delightful feature of Mexican health care is that it seems to actually consider the physical circumstances of being sick. At home, if you wake up after a horrendous night of fever and hacking, you have to put on clothes and drag yourself to a drug store (where you invariably run into your biggest office rival talking to your best-looking neighbor). In Mexico you can call a pharmacy and they will deliver the cough syrup or any non-controlled prescription to you, likely within the hour.

They can also make good suggestions if you do not know exactly what you need. Although medication names are usually very similar in Spanish and English, they are not similar enough to use the English term with Mexican pharmacy technicians who do not speak English (and have frustratingly little imagination).

The Mexico Solution is geared toward the part-time expat. But as so many people test Mexico part-time before moving there permanently to access more affordable health care, I'll go a little further on the topic.

I had a dear friend in San Diego who always said if he ever ran out of money and he needed healthcare, he'd just move to Mexico. I case you might be thinking the same, Mexico is not the place to come when you are sick and out of money. If you are considering participating in Mexico's health care system in an inexpensive, sustained way, you should undertake certain steps several years out from when you will actually need that care. Sadly, you cannot just show up.

Living in Mexico part-time for a few years gives a potential expat the opportunity to put together that plan. You do not necessarily have to live there every day, twelve months a year to participate in the system, but you do need to think ahead.

You will want to consider applying for a *visa temporal*.

A *visa temporal* (a visible step towards residency) opens up a person's health care options in Mexico. In order to get a *visa temporal,* a potential expat needs to provide the Mexican government proof of solvency, a passport, and an address in Mexico. In order to keep it, you must follow the rules carefully about when and how to cross the border and how to renew it. Maintaining the visa requires a bigger annual time commitment to Mexico.

Health Insurance Options

A *visa temporal* or resident visa is required to get enrolled in Mexico's government insurance (*IMMS* and *Seguro Popular*), or to enroll in private insurance with any of the established

Mexican carriers. Many full-time expats with resident visas enroll in the government health care programs as a backup to the health care plan they maintain in the U.S., such as Medicare.

New insurance plans are promoted every year on expat websites. Some claim they will cover pre existing conditions (I'm not sure of their residency requirements). International plans that cover your treatment anywhere, including the U.S., are very expensive. Other policies allow treatment anywhere except the U.S. (which tells you what international insurers think of our health care system).

Expats have the choice of purchasing evacuation insurance, private insurance in Mexico, international/global insurance policies (including or excluding coverage in the U.S.), or sticking with travel insurance and their regular coverage at home. Others have faith they can pay out of pocket for whatever might happen in Mexico and go home for more extensive care covered by other forms of insurance or Medicare.

There is a kaleidoscope of options when it comes to covering yourself as an expat. People elect solutions based on their age, health condition, how long they stay in Mexico every year, their bank account, their tolerance for risk, and their level of confidence in each country's health care system.

When considering Mexican health insurance, you likely will want private insurance unless you can count on having a person take care of you should you become bedridden. Public healthcare in Mexico often does not provide nursing care, even in the hospital. In Mexico, family members are expected to take care of their loved ones. Theirs is a culturally driven solution that works well in Mexico where family networks are extensive.

A few years of living part-time in Mexico will increase your comfort level and confidence in a system that is dressed a little different but still does a great job, many expats say better - than the U.S. With time, you will come to understand the pros and cons of each system in light of your personal needs.

Checklist:

- Most U.S. healthcare policies will not cover you in a foreign country. You will need to purchase travel insurance. Shop carefully, as the prices (and ability to communicate with real people at global companies) vary wildly.

- Upon arrival, ask around for which are the best hospitals in your area should an emergency arise. *This is important.* In an emergency, a doctor may try to take you to a clinic where he has friends. It may not be the best place. Insist on being taken to the hospital that has been recommended by people you trust. Have emergency numbers handy. 911 is the emergency number throughout Mexico. By international law, they have to provide a translator should you request it.

- Do not give any clinic or hospital a credit card until you have established the cost of treatment. Preferably, you will have contacts in Mexico who can check around for you and find out how much your treatment should cost. Pull in your posse. Ask alot of questions about the treatment. This is the time to make sure you have the phone number for the local American embassy or consulate on hand should you need to pull that card.

- If you are applying for a *visa temporal*, the income requirements look straightforward on websites as far as amount. How that income can be earned seems to be open to interpretation by each state's Mexican consulate. The only way to know for sure is to set up an appointment. *Keep track of names of those you talk to, and careful notes.*

- If you get the feeling that no one is giving you a straight answer to a question you have about Mexico, it's because the "answer" depends on the interpretation by the Mexican charged with answering it.

Cooking and Eating Healthy in Mexico

We all know that Mexico has world-class cuisine. Good, inexpensive restaurants are plentiful. Most parts of Mexico have their own specialties. *Enchiladas* are made differently in Veracruz from how they are prepared in other parts of Mexico. *Tlayudas* are the featured best street food in Oaxaca. *Chalupas* are the most representative of Puebla's extensive cuisine. Puerto Vallarta is famous for its *pescado embarazado*. Undoubtedly, sampling all these dishes will be a highlight of your Mexican Experience.

Tortillas are Mexico's biggest culinary gift to the world, full of history and images of the Mexican working class that is fueled by them. No matter how many consumed in a lifetime, the love affair continues. Like a piece of hot fresh crusty bread, chewy and lathered in butter, a fried tortilla satisfies many of the same cravings. Once fried, you can load them up with leftover *anything,* including healthy things like kale and black beans, or even stir-fried vegetables.

I'm particularly enchanted with the clandestine nature of securing fresh tortillas in Mexico. The fresh ones are sold from unmarked coolers in the unlikeliest of places, like OXXO convenience stores. You have to ask for them (which I totally get a kick out of). It goes like this:

Me: Hay tortillas?- (Do you have tortillas?)

Cashier: [With arched eyebrow] You, with your tee-shirt, pasty face, and bobby-pinned hair know of our secret tortillas?

Me: Si... I have sources, and reason to believe you keep some in back.

Cashier: How many do you want, then, American Insurgent? Two pounds?

Me: No, I think six will be plenty.

Cashier: [After furtive discussion with colleagues] That will be seven pesos.

*The tortillas are handed over, still warm, in a paper napkin).

(I finally learned to order them by cost, for example, ten pesos' worth).

Now that I have lived in Mexico this long and know the challenges of everyday cooking as an expat, it surprises me how little shrift the topic is given in books. Eating healthy is always a challenge no matter where you live. In Mexico, the challenge is compounded by the metric system, recipes in Spanish, and unavailability of many of the ingredients common to American/Canadian recipes. My first visit, I almost starved to death (you can read all about why and how to cook healthy food you'll love in Mexico in my cookbook, *Recipes That Translate,* co-authored by food blogger Fabiola Rodriguez.

Any restaurant will be willing to prepare a meal to go. I have taken in my own plates into restaurants to fill rather than their cramming the dinner into those styrofoam cartons. The care that goes into wrapping meals up is touching.

One evening I cabbed to Liverpool, a fairly upscale department store. To my surprise, the store had hired a five-piece mariachi band in full regalia to celebrate the next day's national holiday. Bottled beer was flowing freely throughout the store. Silver platters of hors d'oeuvres offered fresh seafood and elegant sweets were being served by uniformed waiters to an appreciative throng. I loaded up.

Unlike at home where the happy hour buffet is stripped to carrot sticks within an hour, as the store closed the servers were still bringing out fresh platters and filling large cups with beer.

With one of such flagrantly in hand, I left the store and I asked the next cab driver if he'd mind stopping by a taqueria and let me pick up a meal to go. When the one I directed him to was closed, in a move that would have alarmed me three years earlier, without my asking and with no explanation whatsoever he made a U-turn worthy of police pursuit and took me to another one he knew of a few blocks away..

He waited cheerfully in the cab while I received my lovingly-wrapped order of tacos al carbon and a cheese quesadilla. Calling out "Buen Provecho!" he dropped me off at my door. The whole little culinary escapade, cab, food and tip cost a total of $7.

However, you may have noticed this section was included under the title "Keeping Healthy." To be honest, I do not know how healthy typical Mexican dishes are (my Mexican friends tell me none of them are.) Therein lies the challenge. While everyone loves eating out, whether you are at home in the U.S./Canada or Mexico, restaurant fare and street food will likely be far less healthy than cooking at home.

Even Mexicans complain about their ovens. In most of the places I have rented, the ovens are basically a tin box set on top of a red-hot, heavily-breathing heating coil. I have never had one with actual temperatures on the dial. Many ovens in rental apartments have been gas ovens requiring lighting a pilot light. When was the last time you lit an oven's pilot light? I was terrified.

As a result, there are two types of television competitions you will never see - Mexican extreme-sport competitions (Mexicans have more common sense than we do in this regard) and Mexican bread-baking. Don't think you can do any better either. *Tristemente*, you will not be able to make a decent cookie or loaf of bread in Mexico for the same reasons Mexicans cannot.

Ignoring my previously steadfast rule in Mexico, if a Mexican does/doesn't do something that you think would be logical to do/not do, there's a damn good reason for it, I actually believed I could master American baking in a Mexican kitchen. I am that stupid. While I never attempted making bread, I've tried a multitude of baked goods only to be soundly thrashed. Mexicans rely on bakeries.

Organic foods and stores are becoming more and more popular in Mexico. They can be hard to find as stores are tucked away in neighborhoods without much signage or the products themselves are displayed between the serapes and the Osuna tequila. This is where Mexican friends (and Uber drivers) come in handy—to help you find stuff, including organic food.

Resources:

The cookbook *Recipes That Translate* focuses on healthy, easy meals for one to four people than can be prepared in both countries. The book's Ventanas Mexico Pinterest page has a resource board devoted to recipes and cooking tips.

Other websites that are great sources of recipes include Cocina Vital, Kiwilimón (in Spanish but they have helpful videos), Mexican Food Journal, Mexico Cooks, and the cuisine section of Mexconnect.com.

Checklist:

- Finding specialized kitchen utensils can be frustrating and time-consuming, items like hand-held juicers, immersion or stick blender, mallets, apple corers, your favorite chef's knife, are lightweight to pack if you use them frequently.

- As soon as you arrive to Mexico, be on the lookout for signs in the windows of restaurants saying they deliver and grab their delivery menus right then and there. The meal, the tip and the delivery will probably cost less than $15. Like at home, this is a particularly good option for ethnic food. They even deliver smoothies in Mexico.

- Knowing what is *not* available will save you a great deal of time and frustration if you are one of those who puts a lot of effort into meal planning. Take your favorite recipes and check to see if they have any of the following before putting the ingredients on a shopping list in Mexico (Before I had this list, I would come out of grocery stores without all the ingredients to a single dish I'd planned.)

Usually Not Available:

Acorn squash (some squashes will be available in season)

Almond and other nut butters other than peanut butter

Allspice

Artichoke hearts

Applesauce

Arugula (perhaps Sam's Clubs and Walmarts on occasion). It's becoming more popular so keep checking)

Baking potatoes (Idaho)

Barley

Bok Choy

Bolla bread (for pizzas), pita

Blueberries, raspberries

Brussel Sprouts (rare)

Barbeque sauce

Brown rice (it's beginning to appear and you may find precooked in a bag)

Buckwheat

Savoy or red cabbage (you can find green)

Cherries (dried, you can sometimes buy fresh)

Cheddar cheese (they have cheeses called cheddar but typically it is very waxy)

Soft brown sugar (you can grate *perocili* that will do in small quantities, but not for baking that requires 4/1 cup or more)

Cornish hens (except Sam's clubs)

Cannellini beans, although there is a white bean called *alubia*

Chicory

Chutney

Chives

Many types of cheese. (You can usually find Swiss, parmesan, provolone, blue, and goat cheese)

Curry paste

Dried mustard

Edamame (perhaps Sam's Clubs and Walmarts)

Fresh, filled tortellini or pasta (perhaps in Sam's clubs)

Egg noodles (Chinese noodles but not egg noodles) (a tragedy for *coq au vin* and chicken noodle soup fans)

Fennel

Specialty flours

Fish sauce and other sauces for Asian dishes other than soy.

Goji berries

High-quality sandwich meat (most are pressed), with the exception of ham. Mexicans love ham.

Graham cracker pie crusts

Kale (although it's beginning to make appearances) and other hardy greens like swiss chard and collard greens.

Lamb (only at butcher shops)

Lemons, nor bottled lemon juice (again, beginning to be more common). They are beginning to consistently appear in Walmarts.

Lima and colored lentil beans

Molasses

Oat bran

Orzo

Maple syrup (not available according to expert source: the Canadian population)

Kidney beans

Parsnips

Pearl onions or yellow onions (check frozen foods for pearl onions)

Pine nuts

Pesto (premade)

Polenta

Pumpkin seeds (in outdoor markets, not big grocery stores, unless the import isle)

Pumpkin puree

Pomegranate seeds - only whole fruit

Phyllo dough

Radicchio

Rye and other artisanal breads

Split peas

Shallots (you can find them, but not consistently and they are very small)

Slivered almonds (you can find sliced)

Sweet potatoes - seasonal only

Canned tomatoes (when I asked a Mexican about this, he said, "Perhaps because we always have *fresh* tomatoes!")

Tomato paste (specialty shops)

Wild, shitake, and exotic mushrooms other than white and portobello.

Walnuts (sometimes can be found at Sam's Clubs and Walmarts, which have the dubious function as gourmet stores to expats)

Your favorite spice mixes are a good thing to bring in your suitcase. Men particularly often bring their favorite grilling spices with them (I bring celery salt).

<u>Available spices</u>

Azafran - *saffron*

Cloves - *clavo*

Cinnamon - *canela*

Coriander seed (cilantro)

Garlic Powder - *ajo puro*

Vanilla - *vainilla*

Star anise - *anis estillado*

Mint - *menta/hierba buena*

Basil - *albahaca*

Thyme - *tomillo*

Cumin - *comino*

Bay leaf - *hojas laurel*

Ginger - *jengibre*

Oregano - *orégano*

Parsley - *perejil*

Cilantro - *cilantro*

Pepper - *pimiento*

Garlic - *ajo*

Salt and sea salt - *Sal del mar*

Sage - *salvia (*sage looks different in Mexico. It comes, like many herbs, in a cellophane bag. It looks like twigs and broken bay leaves. You have to clean it carefully and mince it. It is also stronger than what you are used to)

Marjoram - *mejorana*

Others that are native to Mexico, like *epazote* (Mexican tea) and *achiote*

Mixed Italian spices and Herbs de Provence are available and these can serve many functions.

Exercise

It is easy to let workouts slide during a vacation. Unfortunately for your exercise goals and health, living in Mexico feels like a vacation every day. You aren't surrounded by the pressure to do it like at home. Mexico has a culture where a woman does not need a size 6 dress to feel attractive. I have worked out religiously since I was 18 years old. My resolve has never before been put to the test the way it has been here.

It takes imagination to stay fit as an expat. Good gyms are scarce. Unless you are in a big city, you have to be one incredibly dedicated gym rat to get used to conditions you'll find in most neighborhood gyms in Mexico. Most expats who exercise at all, walk, often early in the morning (so I hear; I've never personally been up early enough to actually see them).

If your goal is to stay out of both countries' healthcare system, exercise is important. A good home routine is essential in Mexico where outside options are more limited. There are many online workout programs for sale to stream and new ones are produced every day. The best sources for free home workout routines are Pinterest, and YouTube.

Resources:

Exercises are easier to understand with pictures and videos rather than written descriptions. These are some standard body-weight exercises that are consistently recommended for a solid home workout. Enter the exact name of the exercise on YouTube for great demonstration videos. Its search engine is that evolved.

Burpees - a demanding old-stand by that gets easier with time.

Skater jump squats - uses a skater's motion. General fitness.

Push-ups - A 2019 Harvard study says that we can determine our likelihood of dying of cardiovascular disease by how many push-ups we can do. Push-ups can be done in many ways by positioning hands differently.

Planks/side-planks - for upper-body and core strength.

Bird dogs - lower back and balance

Handstand against a wall - We are on our feet all day. Try this for body strength and circulation.

Tricep dips - These only require a chair.

Superman – lower back

Kneeling extensions - For thighs, core and lower back. There are probably a dozen variations.

Deep Squats - leg strength

Lunges/side lunges/spider lunges: Regular, side, and spider lunge - Good for balance and lateral movement as well as leg strength.

Glute bridge - legs, lower back and glutes

Single-leg deadlift - legs and glutes

Wall sits - a skier's standby for thighs

Isometric ballet squats - inner thighs

Isometric front leg raises - legs

Isometric side leg raises from the floor - legs

Abdominal exercises: flutter kicks, crunches, planks.

Yoga in Mexico

When yoga exploded at home two decades ago, thousands of people were inspired to get extensive, often costly training as yoga instructors. Today, even modest gyms in the U.S. provide high-quality classes. Mid-sized cities have dozens of yoga studios.

Not so in Mexico. Far fewer studios exist, and those that do are likely not up to what we have come to expect (although they do not cost 20$ a class either!) have never seen a Pilates class in Mexico. When I do find a yoga class in Mexico, I notice that I make instructors nervous. They assume I cannot speak Spanish and hover over me, which makes me feel decrepit and uncomfortably white.

So it's a good idea to perfect your postures and get good instruction for a home practice if you're thinking of taking it up in Mexico. Personally, I find the *Ashtanga* yoga tradition best when I do not have the support of a class, which is always the case while I'm in Mexico. The postures and breathing are very proscribed, making the order of the postures easier to remember and harder to cheat (not holding the posture long enough).

Stress Reduction: Just Breathe

Between the fire-breathing ovens, dangers of electrical shock, clerks who cock their heads quizzically in that way particular to dogs at your perfect Spanish, and your befuddled, rebellious electronics, it would be a mistake to think that every moment in Mexico will be blissful. Even in Mexico, there will be times you get stressed.

Much has been written about meditation's benefits. Increasingly, Americans are using mediation as a less expensive form of psychotherapy. Even those who struggle with Buddhism's religious concepts are adopting its techniques to relieve stress. The practice of meditation is like a raft that can be used to cross the day's tumultuous waves, no matter which country's shore they are washing up on.

The amount of time to dedicate to mediation is not so much a matter of how many minutes you practice, but rather how long it takes to get to a place of mindful awareness, devoid of racing feelings and thoughts.

In all types, it is common to drift into sleepiness or a blurry stagnated state. Alert yourself when this happens, raise your gaze, breathe out forcefully, straighten your back and bring yourself back to alertness. Divide your awareness between mindfulness of the breath and awareness of your mind and thoughts, letting go of thoughts as they arise.

"The only journey is the one within." - Rainer Maria Rilke

Resources:

The Most Common Methods of Meditation

There are different types of meditation (The Buddha is said to have had 8,900). All, like in yoga, focus on awareness of the breath. These three common methods can be used separately or together if your mind is especially agitated. The important thing is to find whatever combination helps you the most at that time.

Using an object - find an object of natural beauty that inspires you and your own truth. The object can be from your own religious tradition, such as the image of Christ. Fix the object at eye level. Leave your mind quietly at peace. Pay attention to your breath. Bring your attention back to the breath (*prana*), and where you are in the inhalation and exhalation when your mind starts to wander. Many say the most important part of the breathing to focus on (lightly) is in the space between the inhalation and exhalation. Whenever thoughts float in, instead of following them, bring your mind back to the breath.

<u>Reciting a mantra</u> - This technique is used in many faiths, including Christianity, as a way of uniting the mind with the sound of the mantra. Do an online search to find a mantra that resonates with you. Or create your own. The essence of the sound, the way the syllables vibrate, should work directly to produce a sense of calm. Recite it quietly and allow the mantra to roll with your breath until the mantra, your breath, and your awareness become one.

<u>Watching the breath</u> - Rest your attention mindfully on your breath. Counting to the breath helps when you are new to practice. Each time your mind wanders, you return to the breath and start the count over. Notice the breath as it moves through the different parts of your body.

If using the three methods together, you begin by resting your gaze on the object, then reciting the mantra. Once you have practiced with the two methods long enough for your mind to be somewhat calmed, you can turn your attention again to the breath. Using the three together can be really helpful when you are especially agitated. With the right form of meditation, the mind can unknot itself and experience calmness.

Checklist:

- Yoga mats are cheap in Mexico (no reason to pack them). I have bought them for less than 200 pesos (about $18 dollars) at Walmart. If you do pack one, buy a foldable rather than rolled mat.

- Meditation podcasts and websites are very popular as they can be downloaded and accessed on a phone. Some good ones are Insight Timer (Insighttimer.com) which is free, and Calm (calm.com).

Chapter Twelve: Life is Better in Spanish

How to unpack and lay out before you the whole thrilling experience of speaking another language? Of all the goals I have set, learning Spanish has given me the greatest joy, even when I still have so far to go before being satisfied. Even a little Spanish opens whole new worlds in Mexico. Without it, you pay more and laugh less.

Before concluding that I likely have inherent ability, far from it. My grades from a year in Spain as a college student actually brought my final overall grade point average *down*. All I have ever had going for me was desire. Fortunately, that's all you need.

From the beginning, I have used hostage situations like cab and Uber rides to test out new vocabulary and verb conjugations on unwitting victims. Occasionally a Spanish word, like *batiburrillo* or *chida,* haunts me to a point that I ask relative strangers to explain it. Mexicans, regardless of social status, love their language as much as I do. I have experienced everyone from beach lifeguards to well-known economists get fired up explaining its wonders. Asking about words you do not understand is a terrific icebreaker.

Learning Spanish is like carrying a crossword puzzle or scrabble board that you can whip out like a party favor on a moment's notice when you are bored. With a new language, a little bit of adventure follows you around wherever you go, such as the time I accidentally asked an eighty-year-old if he liked to dress in leather (teary-eyed, it was hard for us to continue the conversation after that).

Expat social circles evolve differently when you live in a country where you do not speak the primary language at native level. Rather than along socioeconomic lines, expat social circles are delineated by language. In a way, relationships are more authentic because symbols like profession or neighborhood you live in do not bear as much freight.

You are an expat, and that alone gives you automatic membership to that club. How far you go from there will depend on your Spanish. Language abilities will determine the scope of your social life. Social circles fall into these categories:

- Expats who won't learn Spanish

- Expats who speak some Spanish

- Expats who are bilingual

- Mexicans who are bilingual

- Mexicans who speak some English (You both are learning a second language. You speak to them in Spanish. They answer you in English. At some point you realize how funny this is.)

- Mexicans who speak no English (After all, it is their country.)

Many times, when a couple moves to a Spanish-speaking country, one person will embrace learning the language (often because they have a head start on it in school or with relatives) while the other gives up after they have learned enough to navigate day to day. Most people come with some intention to learn, but drop out once they have made expat friends and established a social life in Mexico. Such a pity.

As it has been relayed to me by expat spouses who do not learn any Spanish, nothing is more demoralizing than finally being invited to a social event in Mexico with your fluent spouse and not understanding a word anyone is saying.

In spite of their best intentions, gradually such couples (where only one learns) find themselves limiting their social life to other expats rather than boring the non-Spanish-speaking spouse. Both subsequently miss out on one of the most gratifying aspects of living in Mexico—sharing the culture.

It is natural to feel self-conscious speaking in the presence of anyone who speaks the second language better, even a spouse. What if, God forbid, you live in a foreign-speaking country and something happens to the bilingual spouse? What if you have to get your partner to the emergency room (*Socorro!*).

The dynamics between couples do not always make them ideal practice partner. If your spouse is bilingual, it can feel like you'll never talk like they do. If they are learning too, it's rather like when as a ski instructor, I used to watch from the ski lift as below me one spouse with three lessons under his belt shouted out fevered instructions to the spouse who'd had none.

If you do not feel you are getting anywhere practicing with a spouse, don't do it. Take private lessons online. Recruit free Skype practice partners from one of several terrific websites students join to find practice partners. Carve out the first hour or two of the day and/or schedule a specific time, like after your daily workout, to achieve the consistency necessary to become conversant.

Knowing Spanish makes life easier.

The more Spanish you speak, the deeper and wider will be your social safety net. Other reasons to commit an hour or two a day to language-learning include:

1. You will save money. When you reach a conversational level, you will be able to ask Mexicans rather than expats what they pay for a plumber, a dentist, a piece of jewelry, or for rent in a neighborhood you want to live in. Believe me, their numbers will be different.

2. You will have a lot more fun. Mexicans are the warmest, most social people in the world. Mexican friends are what make life in Mexico such a positive adventure, as they show you their haunts and how they celebrate special days.

   Everyday incidents that would normally be just mildly amusing can be hilarious when you factor in the language variable. Unlike Americans, who rarely take under their tent anyone with less than excellent English, Mexicans are much more accepting of the occasional confusion in communication inherent in having foreign friends. With a little effort, you can be *their* adventure.

3. You will better understand the culture in modern terms. Many popular preconceptions about Mexicans and Mexican culture are dead wrong, lingering from thirty years ago or more. With Spanish, you can ask them questions about their culture personally, rather than hear theories from other expats.

4. You will be safer. You will be able to ask for help, advice, and the way out of a dicey neighborhood.

5. You will be more independent. You will not have to depend on finding bank clerks, bureaucrats, or workmen who speak English to conduct daily business transactions.

6. You can research subjects online and get better information in Spanish when in Mexico. Being able to mine information from Spanish-language websites is very valuable in cross-checking information on crime in an area. There are services and businesses you will never know exist if you cannot do a search in Spanish. Reviews of restaurants and services are in Spanish, and these critiques are the best way of getting a feel for a performance or a menu.

7. Your travel choices will broaden as you will be able to navigate any Spanish-speaking country or any small town in Mexico without being restricted to tourist areas, which is the *best* tourism there is.

I am still far from bilingual, having taken the language up again after thirty years of complete absence. When I focus, my Spanish is quite good, punctuated by moments of brilliance. When I get really emotional or excited, I might as well be speaking Mandarin. Yet, learning Spanish has made a profound difference in my daily life here.

Language shapes personality

Articles about why you should learn a second language never discuss the opportunity it gives you to build a whole new language environment for someone else to inhabit and respond to. If you are aware of how you construct your "linguistic environment" by the words you choose, you have a powerful tool to reshape how you are perceived and perceive.

The words you use are who you are to others. Think about that. My favorite example of this profunity was the story I read about a German learning Italian. His wife preferred him "in Italian," where he was a completely different person from when he spoke his native tongue.

Taking this cue, I have always focused on learning a number of variations for positive words in Spanish and have a very short list of negative ones, just enough for a push-back emergency.

I have a theory that while I may not be a better person in Mexico, I express myself as a better person. I have given myself fewer options for speaking in negative terms. The few times I have wanted to tell a Mexican off, I have not been able to get much further than "*malo*"(bad). It's really hard to anger someone with the word "*malo*." They will just roll their eyes (which is better in the long run anyway).

On the other hand, having a dozen ways to say "beautiful," or "I am grateful," or "That's awesome" has served me quite well. With so many of these variations of positive words and phrases, I am considered wonderfully fluent, as well as a nicer person than I probably am.

Your Brain on Spanish

If none of these intriguing possibilities motivate you to pick up some Spanish, do it for your brain. Researchers compare the benefits of speaking two languages with weightlifting at a gym. The bilingual has to lift more weight than the monolingual because bilinguals experience mental competition within and between both their languages while listening to speech. The bilingual brain is stronger than it would be without the second language because it has been mentally working out. Tellingly, speaking Spanish for extended periods as a beginner is physically exhausting.

The workout analogy is not metaphorical. A frequently cited Swedish study showed parts of the brain associated with memory (such as the hippocampus and cerebral cortex) physically grow, like muscles, when stimulated regularly during the mental workout a second language gives you.

A great deal has been written about the cognitive benefits of learning a second language. Specific to learning a language as an older adult, studies have shown that it increases the brain's plasticity, its ability to grow and make new connections. By keeping different parts of the brain active as we age, learning a new language helps keep cognition sharp and the neuronal connections clipping along. Learning a second language can keep us "thinking" young.

Learning grammar, memorizing vocabulary, and struggling with verb conjugations have positive effects on your everyday cognitive retention—i.e., your memory. Although learning a language will not totally halt the onset of Alzheimer's and other forms of dementia in susceptible individuals, according to studies, it can fend it off for up to five years and has been shown to be more effective than any currently prescribed drugs.

Studies have shown that pleasure reading is not enough to maintain mental acuity. Don't become one of those expats with a flabby brain! It needs a harder workout. If planning to live in Mexico in retirement mode, learning Spanish provides the perfect mental workout you need, no matter how comfortable you could make your life in Mexico without it.

Learning is more accessible than ever.

For the first time, people no longer need to travel to a foreign country to become fluent in its language, as so many free online tools exist to learn. In my language journey, I got so excited about all the free tools available that I wrote a book curating them, the *Interactive Guide to Learning Spanish Free Online*.

YouTube Videos and Netflix series in Spanish help with listening skills and grammar. There are websites devoted to helping you practice writing. You can choose Spanish-language music stations on Pandora or Spotify. You can hire Skype teachers or recruit free practice partners on Skype. You can order easy-vocabulary books in Spanish from your library or Amazon. The tools are endless.

Structure your learning.

Many people get so excited about learning that they spend a lot of money on expensive language programs they find on the first few pages of a Google search. After a few weeks they quit. Many of these programs are not that great (although their advertising is), and most students get bored quickly.

Grammar lessons, vocabulary tools, and listening and speaking tools are all available free online. Explore them before buying an expensive comprehensive program. *Set your study habits first with the free tools.* Establishing the discipline to study is more important than having an expensive program that collects dust.

Watching movies on Netflix and listening to music in Spanish are less work, more fun, and predictably, much less effective according to experts and student surveys. View them more as rewards for the harder work you do (the exception to this might be Spanish-language telenovelas if they are used in a deliberate, systematic way, with flashcards and repetition, rather than passively viewed). You can only get so far without learning grammar, and bad habits that you pick up by listening are hard to break. YouTube hosts many lesson sites that cover grammar.

MeetUps and Similar Practice Groups

A good first step to speaking is regular, consistent attendance at free language-practice groups like MeetUps in your city. They usually meet in coffee shops and places like Whole Foods. They attract all kinds of people, and can even provide good connections, as most members have spent time in Spanish-speaking countries, especially Mexico.

While the meetings can be intimidating at first, their main advantage is to force you to speak, the hardest thing to do as a beginner. Overcoming self-consciousness with a supportive group where everyone is learning will teach you to forge ahead, even if you haven't gotten the past tense down yet. You are more likely to do your own studying at home if you attend consistently.

Even if you end up spending time conversing with students who know even less Spanish than you do, the biggest advantage of these groups is getting you used to, comfortable even, making mistakes.

The degree of discomfort and avoidance a person feels in attending group practices is usually in direct proportion to how much they should attend them. When you no longer care about making mistakes, you have overcome the number one hurdle to learning to speak a second language fluently. From there the world opens up.

Too many people postpone going to such groups, telling themselves they want to learn a little more grammar or vocabulary first before attending. The flaw in this logic is pretty obvious. You don't learn Spanish in order to speak it. You speak Spanish in order to learn it.

Speaking every week will give you far more motivation to go back to your studies in vocabulary and grammar. You also will be able to prioritize what you study after repeatedly coming up empty on certain topics (which likely will not include dressing in leather.)

Every practice group has its own personality, attracting older or younger members depending on time and venue. As an older student, I found that groups with more members around my age tended to be more inviting. As much as I hate to generalize, after several years of attending many different groups, I found that older members tend to be more focused on their language goals and more supportive of same-age peers (maybe they are all thinking about moving to Mexico and not about their next date).

Once in Mexico, try to find English/Spanish group exchanges. These groups will be attended both by Mexicans learning English as well as expats. They are a great way to make Mexican friends.

Professional instructors

In surveys by language teaching sites, out of all the methods of learning, students felt they learned the most from private teachers. Private lessons from a professional teacher can get expensive. My personal experience is that a conscientious, free-practice exchange partner can do as well teaching you as 90 percent of the professional teachers on online sites. Both of you only need to commit to helping each other with exercises and resources, all to be found free online.

Online professional Spanish instructors are marvelous people. They are enthusiastic and personable. Their challenge is that they have many students and can rarely focus on the progress of a single student. Even with tools, the lessons tend to be fragmented. You can spend a great deal of money trying to find one with whom you have good chemistry and is consistently organized for your specific needs.

If you go the route of paying professional teachers online, insist that your teacher has the means to measure your progress and tests you (studies show you learn three times more taking tests than you do simply studying). They should have exercises and educational tools. They should be ready for specific tasks if you desire, like improving your facility with compound verbs or the subjunctive mood, skills harder to master with only daily Spanish conversation and studying. Work with the instructor on how to best prepare to teach you effectively.

Do not let a professional online teacher with professional rates get away with simply conversing with you. Many will try. You do not need to pay professional rates just to talk. To only converse, hire community tutors instead. There are excellent (fun!) tutors for less than 10$ an hour (italki is one of several great sites), whereas a professional teacher will cost between 12$ and 25$ (or more) an hour. It may not sound like that much more money, but it adds up when it takes months (at least) to learn a language.

Group Classes in Schools and Community Centers

In a high-quality group Spanish class, the teacher is a facilitator, getting students to talk with exercises like role-playing and thought-provoking scenarios, not by giving lectures. Classes of this caliber are extremely rare, most often limited to specific certification programs.

Typical group classes offered in U.S. community colleges or Mexican cities are often excruciating. They may sound like a bargain but score very low on effectiveness. Most teachers think you will learn by hearing *them* speak. You can get plenty of that watching YouTube videos or podcasts in Spanish. *You* need to speak.

Even with less than a dozen students, group classes are too large to get speaking practice in unless you have that exceptional instructor. (I learned this early in Mexico; after spending ten minutes discussing the Spanish word for "church veil," I decided this was not the vocabulary rabbit hole I wanted to go down).

Free Online Language Partners

Skype is truly a game-changer for mid-intermediate and up language students. The oldest and best sites to find older learners for Skype practice are My Language Exchange, Conversation Exchange, and Language for Exchange, which have deep benches of fellow students over forty years old, as well as the bright shiny faces of hundreds of younger enthusiasts.

In a Skype practice with a language-exchange partner, you typically speak English half the time and Spanish the other half (although I have had partners who wanted to maximize speaking time, so we both only spoke our second languages). Most prefer the video feature where you can see one another, but you can turn off the camera and go simply with audio too (although I have found that those who do not use the camera never last. I don't know why. Accountability?). Give a new practice partner at least a few sessions to warm up. If you are the shy one, go in with a few icebreakers of your own.

Prepare for the first language-exchange sessions by having open-ended questions prepared that encourage longer responses ("Tell me about where you live"). Share resources with your partners. Find easy, interesting stories they can read to you should the conversation falter

(Medium.com is a good place to find easy, short stories). Exchange means they need to get as much as you do from the practice.

Keeping a full stable of reliable language-exchange partners with whom you click initially takes time and effort. Partners fall off and you have to recruit replacements. If you are trying to practice every day during the week, you will need about five practice partners in order to practice speaking Spanish thirty minutes a day. Consistency is important. As with MeetUps, you will find that the conversations motivate the rest of your study efforts.

Sharing a hobby like learning a language is a bonding experience. Students typically develop meaningful friendships with their exchange partners. After all, you are conversing every week for months, even years.

My language partners and I share YouTube music videos, movie recommendations, and all kinds of interesting insights. If we do not have anything new to talk about, we whip out some exercises or articles to translate together. All this is free except for the 6$ a month you will need to pay every now and then when you need to recruit new partners.

Paid Online Tutors

An alternative to recruiting free exchange partners is hiring a conversation partner through sites like italki. For less than $10 an hour, you can hire tutors who will simply converse with you. The advantage is that the hour can be all about you, without worrying about what they are getting out of it.

Online tutors are also recommended for those who are only beginning to speak when you are not yet fluent enough to maintain Skype conversations in Spanish. You will need to study verb conjugations and basic vocabulary before you get started. A paid tutor's job is to lead the conversation. Their rating depends on your satisfaction. If you are a rote beginner and cannot find a practice MeetUp group in your area or feel uncomfortable reaching out to free language exchange partners, this is a great way to go.

Life is frequently a trade-off of time versus money. You can pay a community tutor 8$ a day, five days a week, and receive a full hour each day of strictly Spanish conversation, no English. That adds up to 160$ a month, yet might be worth it if your time frame for moving to Mexico is short and you do not have time to recruit free practice partners.

Taking the Big sStep: Conversing with Mexicans...in Mexico

Once you meet a few nice people in Mexico, think about inviting one to an activity that doesn't focus too much on conversation but still provides time to practice, like a play, concert, or the movies.

While I had opportunities to go out on dates in Mexico my first year, I am grateful now that I made the early decision to focus on same-sex friendships first (the same can probably be said of moving to any new city.) Same-sex friends in Mexico will eventually be more helpful in introducing you to a broader circle of people in their social and family circles as your language skills improve. Those women are with me still. Take the long view.

If your goal is practice, do not invite those who speak English better than you do Spanish - unless you do not mind speaking English all night. Unless strict ground rules are set about dividing the time between speaking Spanish and speaking English (hard to enforce in a social situation), whomever speaks the second language best will get all the practice.

If you speak Spanish better than Juan speaks English, Spanish will dominate the evening. If Alejandro's English is better than your Spanish, English will dominate. Even a small advantage eventually puts the other out of the game completely. Focus on developing some relationships with Mexicans whose English is worse than your Spanish if you really want to learn the language.

Don't give up.

It is completely natural to get frustrated when learning a language. Expect it. With time you will discover words in Spanish that represent an idea or condition that required many words in English or can't be translated, period. These are delightful, tiny apertures through which you can view another culture. You can learn at any age (several of my favorite Skype practice partners are well over sixty, only started a few years ago, and speak well).

Like any sport or mentally challenging hobby, being a beginner language student is grueling at first. Like a good golf swing, a few victories will keep you going until you have developed a full-fledged superpower.

My most memorable experiences in Mexico invariably are those in which I have been speaking Spanish. Sure, you can make do without Spanish in Mexico, but with so many terrific free tools available and so many benefits, why would you want to?

I was walking dogs for a friend of mine at night and passed a group of teenagers. They appeared to be regular upper-middle-class kids. In spite of that, one of the teenage girls peeled off the group, approached me and aggressively asked me why I was walking the dogs so late at night.

Without Spanish, I might not have understood the teenager's question and certainly would have been intimidated. With Spanish, I could cheerfully tell her I wasn't too afraid of being attacked while holding a steaming bag of dog poop in my hand (I think I actually said *boiling* poop). She laughed a little nervously, and immediately bounded back to her group.

Resources:

The *Interactive Guide to Learning Spanish Free Online* lists hundreds of free resources along with giving you live links and lesson plans organized according to level. You can use the lessons or create your own new ones every day. The book is supported by "Website of the Week" on the Ventanas Mexico website, with a link to my favorite free tool of the week.

For those who absolutely do not want to learn Spanish—Free "Survival Spanish" tools include David Reilly's: *Spanish Made Easy* and *Learn Spanish Survival Guide* by Survival Spanish. The search term "learn Spanish survival guide" will bring up numerous tools. YouTube is also awash with learning videos.

Checklist:

- Google Translate has come a long way. In addition to translating whole sentences as well as words, its camera feature will translate written words on signs, menus, wherever. A hand-held translation device has also been introduced that will radically change people's comfort level in foreign travel. Other good tools are linguee.com and reverso.com

- It is really common for people speaking English in Mexico to speak too loudly in public spaces. They can hear you.

Chapter Thirteen: Timeline for Moving to Mexico Part-time

The tasks necessary to move to Mexico part-time, if spread out and scheduled, will be less overwhelming. Discipline yourself to do tasks as early as they can be done (it's the tasks that have no deadlines that trip you up). Otherwise, they pile up and can make your last few weeks in the U.S. (the weeks you most want to spend time with friends and family), much less enjoyable than they should be.

Eighteen Months Out

- ○ Move all U.S. recurring bills to auto-pay.

- ○ Save money for initial outlays if necessary (you recoup your money over time in Mexico)

- ○ Analyze phone plans (in both countries) and estimate data usage. Research major carriers for Mexico/Canada/U.S. plans.

- ○ Apply for a passport (or renew if necessary). If applying for a *visa temporal,* begin gathering necessary documentation according to the consulate website, including proof of income documentation. Set appointment with nearest Mexican consulate.

- ○ Start compiling entertainment lists (playlists, book lists, podcasts). It's natural to leave the "optional" tasks for your free time later. Do not. The delayed tasks will accumulate, taking all your free time.

○ Decide on whether to keep a car in the U.S. If not decide on the process to sell it. If the car is leased, see if you can swap the lease. This takes time, a year or more sometimes.

○ Determine how you will rent out your current U.S. home or apartment (Study housing laws in your state). If you rent an apartment and it would not be attractive for a rental, consider moving to one that would be.

○ Attend Spanish practice groups (MeetUps and similar) consistently. Set up (and keep!) a daily study schedule.

○ If you plan on working. Do remote work research. Try to work remotely in the U.S for a while as a test. Research companies that hire remote workers. See if you can work a few days remotely with your current employer.

One Year Out

○ Look up medicines and prescriptions you'll need in Spanish. Have health records translated into Spanish and put on a flashdrive.

○ Begin networking with Facebook groups and other social media in your Mexican town or city of interest. Keep a spreadsheet to organize systematic contact.

○ Make copies and laminate important documentation (passport, birth certificate, FMM documentation, driver's license).

○ Select and purchase items to make U.S. place more attractive to renters.

○ Begin paring down possessions as much as humanly possible.

○ Determine your purpose in Mexico (even if it's to find a new one).

Six Months Out

- ○ Finalize city and neighborhood in Mexico you want to live in. Begin networking or contacting realtors for places to rent.

- ○ Apply for credit cards *that have no foreign transaction fees* for use in Mexico and provide car rental insurance as part of their coverage.

- ○ Establish a back-up bank account in bank separate from your primary bank. Compile a notebook of pin numbers and emergency numbers should your card get lost or stolen.

- ○ Get a library card from your closest major library. If you have not already, check out a few books online.

- ○ Determine what small kitchen utensils (chef's knives, apple corer) you may need to pack. Purchase a paper Spanish dictionary. Purchase lightweight exercise equipment such as bands, foldable yoga mat and/or a jump rope.

- ○ Consider small gifts for Mexican friends.

- ○ Research rental concierges in Mexico (it may take time to find them) and develop a list.

- ○ (*If Only I Had a Place* has listings)

Three Months Out

- ○ Run an ad or post other listings to seek a tenant for your U.S. home or apartment.

- ○ Begin more arduous cleaning tasks that you might normally do once or twice a year.

- ○ Get any training for hobbies or work that you cannot get through online courses (like yoga training).

- Review the functionality of all electronic devices. Purchase extra brand-name chargers and any accessories you might need. Consider extra electronics by asking yourself, "If this were to break, how would it affect my life in Mexico?"

- Begin trip planning (do not purchase airline tickets until you have secured a tenant). If driving, research routes, stops, and hotels (If you have a pet, you will need to find those hotels that take them). If staying in hotels in Mexico, purchase a portable carbon monoxide alarm.

- Decide where your mail will be forwarded. Perhaps a trusted friend or a mail service that can scan and send your mail to you electronically.

- Determine internet and data needs. Do you need to purchase a portable hotspot?

Thirty Days Out

- Thoroughly check references of all prospective tenants of your U.S. home or apartment and select your tenant. Deposit security check.

- Check travel advisories for Mexico (particularly if driving).

- Confirm Mexico rental arrangements and airline tickets. Hire concierge in Mexico to look at the rental you have selected.

- If taking pets, visit the vet to make sure they have proper documentation of required vaccinations.

- Research and purchase travel insurance (health only).

- Begin packing personal possessions for storage.

- Turn travel plans in with your bank.

○ Complete safety check of car and repairs if driving. Create manifesto of everything you plan to carry across the border.

One Week Out

○ Deliver personal items to storage or have boxes picked up by moving company.

○ Finish final cleaning of apartment for renter.

○ Make final arrangements with the tenant for pick up of keys, codes, and written agreement to terms of stay.

○ Confirm travel arrangements a final time.

○ Complete packing several days before leaving.

○ Make arrangements for getting to the airport if flying.

○ See all your friends. Buy them a round.

Conclusion

To live creative lives we have to borrow, steal and repurpose ideas from a vast range of sources. Nothing gives you a fresh supply of experiences and influences to pull from like living in two countries. Each passage leaves a piece of itself with you. Different surroundings bring out different qualities in us. How we respond tells us a little more about ourselves.

I do not know with certainty if I will ever move to Mexico full-time, although the odds increasingly favor it. The American healthcare crisis, foreboding trends in housing, income inequality, and the rising cost of living in the U.S. as measured against it are pushing a wave of Americans to kinder shores.

Every year I better understand Mexico as a place where I could retire one day with more grace, comfort and dignity than I could ever expect at home. For all the conveniences of big-city life in America, the voices and language of Mexico pulls me closer every day. The sense of flow they impart sustains itself for long periods – days, weeks even - in a way I cannot achieve in the U.S anymore.

At home, I am struck by convenience and abundance. In Mexico, it is the people who fill me with wonder (although the scenery isn't bad either). How can they be so patient with the inconveniences? How do they find so much time to spend with one another and their families doing what matters? How can there be so many sixty-five-year-old women out dancing in the middle of the night?

I think and write a lot about fear. I'm scared of many things and new ones arise all the time, constantly testing me. That is what fears are there for. I don't always pass these tests, but in Mexico the sleepless nights are far fewer, worries often blown away by the sound of the palm trees waving outside my window.

Many expats have written about being forced to return unwillingly to the U.S., shaking them from the comfort zone they've found in Mexico. Someday that might be my new overarching fear - the fear of having to go back.

In arranging housing in Guadalajara for a business trip I had found a couple through social networking who were going to California for the Christmas holidays during the same period. They were looking for someone to watch their place (I would be paying rent, but the amount sounded secondary).

A Mexican friend had recently moved with her family to Guadalajara. I was excited that I'd be able to see her and shared with her how wonderful the couple sounded. She instructed me to call the woman and ask for her permission to give her (my friend) her phone number, my friend's plan being to make a social call on her with her adult son.

At home, such a thing would be considered outrageous, almost an intrusion. Imagine calling an absolute stranger and inviting yourself over to make sure they were good enough to board your friend.

My friend is an accomplished artist. Her son is a handsome masters graduate who had just found an engineering position in Guadalajara. They not only spoke much better Spanish, they are charming, attractive (and better dressed), than me. In closer consideration, I realized that their meeting would do nothing but increase my cache. If the four of them were to meet, my only worry need be that I would be a disappointment in comparison.

Feeling that little shift under me that I get in Mexico when I feel cultural plates rubbing together, I called the new contact and asked if my friend might call her regarding a visit in advance of my stay. My friend would like to meet her.

I held my breath. With warmth and alacrity, the woman not only agreed for me to give my friend her number but also gave me the distinct sense that indeed this was a perfectly normal, natural request, Mexicana a Mexicana. The two couples, my friend and her husband and my new Guadalajara contacts, met for dinner two weeks before my arrival.

And this, my friends, is why I love Mexico and Mexicans. Weeks before I arrived to Guadalajara, these four people had already spun out another strand of that sticky social and cultural web that keeps us, like spiders, clinging stubbornly to our lives in Mexico.

"Thanks for reading! If you enjoyed this book or found it useful, I'd be very grateful if you'd post a short review on Amazon. Your support really does make a difference!

Kerry Baker lives in Denver, Colorado and Mazatlán, Mexico. In addition to the Ventanas Mexico blog (www.ventanasmexico.com), she is the author of the *Interactive Guide to Learning Spanish Free Online* (a curation of the best free tools on the web, organized by level with interactive links), and *If Only I Had a Place* (a book on how to rent well in Mexico), and *Recipes That Translate,* a cookbook for expats co-authored by Mexican food blogger Fabiola Rodriguez Licona

For future information related to the subject of this book, subscribe at www.ventanasmexico.com

Made in the USA
Las Vegas, NV
15 March 2022